This book is an amazing testimony of how ⟨...⟩ Paige's story will not only leave you shaken, but it will motivate you to step out and live differently. Her story has the potential to wake up an entire generation for the glory of God. Read on and become that generation.

—Mike Blackaby,
speaker and coauthor of *When Worlds Collide*

Many books *inspired* me, but only a few provided the rough shake needed for radical life transformation. This was one of the few. Paige's passionate plea to her generation is heart-wrenching, humorous, uncomfortable, and at its heart, unavoidably convicting. When I reluctantly finished, I was no longer at the same place spiritually as I when I began. Life is much too short to spend sleepwalking; we *need* a wakeup call—and with this essential book, Paige has given us one.

—Daniel Blackaby,
speaker and coauthor of *When Worlds Collide*

All of us have stories to tell, but few of us recognize their power. In *Wake Up, Generation,* Paige Omartian delivers a fresh and fervent challenge to a generation rendered immobile by apathy. She empowers us all to rise up and join the greatest Story ever told.

—Constance Rhodes,
Founder and CEO of FINDINGbalance;
author of *The Art of Being: Reflections on the Beauty and Risk of Embracing Who We Are*

Paige's book is a must-read. It is a clarion call to live the life God calls us to live in a world where so many are either bored or simply going through the motions. My prayer is that this book will find its way into the hands of young people who will be inspired to serve and live authentic lives. We serve an amazing God and I am thankful to Paige for her willingness to be used by Him to help inspire others and, in the process, help to heal a hurting world.

—David Williams,
President and CEO, Make-A-Wish Foundation

I wish I'd read this book when I was younger. No doubt it would have saved me many painful lessons! Paige inspires and enlightens us through this book to find the source of our identity and ignite a real, relevant, and radical sense of purpose. The practical applications throughout the book will help you walk out your own story and clearly see through the lies the world tells us about ourselves. I could not recommend this book enough—everyone needs to hear this miraculous story and should expect a real life change through it.

—Robert Beeson,
President and CCO, BEMA Media,
founder of Essential Records

We live in a time in which there are so many things to keep us occupied and entertained, and yet we are still falling asleep, missing the very work we have been called to do. Paige speaks to us in a way that catches our attention and "wakes us and shakes us," up and out. This is not a how-to book but it is a have-done book. Her story of resilience propels evens the sleepiest to *wake up.*

—Jamie Grace,
winner of the 2012 Dove Award
for New Artist of the Year

WAKE UP GENERATION

PAIGE OMARTIAN

HARVEST HOUSE PUBLISHERS
EUGENE, OREGON

Cover by Koechel Peterson & Associates, Inc., Minneapolis, Minnesota

WAKE UP, GENERATION
Copyright © 2012 by Paige Omartian
Published by Harvest House Publishers
Eugene, Oregon 97402
www.harvesthousepublishers.com

Library of Congress Cataloging-in-Publication Data
Omartian, Paige, 1990-
Wake up, generation / Paige Omartian.
    p. cm.
ISBN 978-0-7369-4577-6 (pbk.)
ISBN 978-0-7369-4578-3 (eBook)
1. Omartian, Paige, 1990- 2. Spiritual biography. 3. Healing. I. Title.
BL73.O43A3 2012
248.8'3—dc23

2011048023

To my parents, Donna and Gary Armstrong.
This book is because of you—
your invaluable lessons,
your sacrifices,
your godly character,
and your prayers.

ACKNOWLEDGMENTS

This book is the result of God's goodness to me in the form of many wonderful people who deserve my deepest gratitude.

To the Harvest House team…you are a gift! Bob Hawkins, Jr., Terry Glaspey, LaRae Weikert, and my wonderful editor, Kathleen Kerr, I am so grateful that you stepped out in faith and believed with me in this vision. It is a privilege to be working with such godly people.

To my awesome agents at Reclaim Management, Rebeca Seitz and Steven Feldman—thank you for journeying with me and blessing me with your amazing creativity and support! Jessica Dotta, thank you for being the first person to read my book and help me raise the bar.

To those who took my dreams seriously and helped me get started— Diane Sheets, Jeff Risden, Robert Beeson, Brad Mathias, and Kevan Cyka. Constance Rhodes, you were the first author to take me under your wing. I'm grateful for your sweet vulnerability and friendship.

To Shawna Kirk, your work with Compassion International makes my heart overflow. Thank you for giving me the opportunity to see the world in a way I never had before.

To the friends who let me use their precious stories in these chapters— thank you. Your lives are a walking example of this book.

To those who stood by my side during my battle with cancer, God used your encouragement to keep my spirit alive.

To the Make-A-Wish Foundation, you started it all with the wish you granted me.

To my new family, the Omartians…Stormie, you have showered me with love and graciousness from day one. I am inspired by you, blessed by you, and forever indebted to you for far too many gifts that I could never repay. Michael, Mandy, and Dallas, you bring me such joy! Thank you for all your prayers, encouragement, and laughs during this process. I love you!

To my wonderful parents and family, you've been with me through it all. Mom, Dad, Scot, Marie, Jenna, Brian, Kali, Josh, and the newest members of our family...Savanna, Scott, and little Ben! Each of you have taught me so much. Thank you for your undying love and support. I couldn't possibly love you more.

To Chris, my heart's new home. Who could have known that as I wrote this book I'd also be planning the greatest day of my life—the day I married you! Thank you for saying "I do" to our journey together. You prayed me through each chapter of this book, just as I know you'll pray us through each new chapter of our lives.

To my precious Lord...what is there to say? *Your* name should be on the cover of this book, because I couldn't have written a word without You. Thank You for entrusting me with this message. Every breath is for and because of You.

Last but not least—to my little "coauthor" and kitty, Kiana, who snuggled on my lap as I slaved over every word. I have a feeling her sweet companionship kept me sane as I wrote this book.

CONTENTS

FOREWORD

The first time I met Paige, her reputation preceded her. She had previously worked with my son, Christopher, on her record album—she is a professional singer, he is a record producer, and they are both songwriters. During that time, Chris often talked with me about Paige and her amazing life story and near-death experience. Time and again he mentioned what an exceptional person she is. I was intrigued.

Soon after that my husband started coming home from rehearsals for a concert series for young people, with which he had some involvement, raving about a young woman they had hired to be the main speaker. She was a singer/songwriter who had an amazing life story to tell and a great message. It was, again, Paige.

So by the time Chris invited me to dinner to meet Paige, I knew who she was. We hit it off immediately and had much to talk about. Paige told me more about her story—which is remarkably compelling—and her vision for what she knew God was calling her to do. I asked if she had given any thought to writing a book about what God had done in her life; she told me she had already started writing it.

I requested that she send me anything of what she had written that was finished enough for me to read. The following week she gave me the table of contents and a few chapters. As I read them I was greatly impressed by what a good writer she is, and at such a young age. I couldn't wait to read the rest of the book.

Paige agreed to let me tell my publisher at Harvest House about her and when I did, they immediately asked that she send what she had written so far, along with a synopsis of the book. She showed me the package she had put together for them and I could not imagine that the people at Harvest House wouldn't be as pleased as I was. And they certainly were! Right away they wanted to meet with her, and not long afterward she had signed a contract with them.

During the following year, while she was finishing the book, my husband and I fell in love with Paige. So did our family and friends. So did our publishing company. And so did our son, Chris! He and Paige were married a few months ago and I have never seen him so happy. The day before their wedding I was struck with the fact that I had been praying for Christopher's wife from the time he was born. I prayed that God would guide and protect her and prepare her for all He had for her to do. I realized that I had been praying for her during the entire time she was fighting for her life—in the hospital and throughout her miraculous recovery. I found it very moving to know that I'd had that connection with her before I ever knew her.

We couldn't be more thrilled to have Paige as part of our family. We love her like a daughter and her wonderful family as our own. She is truly God's gift to us. The greatest thing about Paige is not how talented, gifted, and beautiful she is, but more importantly how godly, devoted, faithful, loving, gracious, sweet, fun, and funny she is. She is tiny, yet formidable, and she has the biggest heart for the Lord and for others. She deeply cares about the young people of her generation.

That's why I know this book will be of tremendous benefit to you as you read her powerful message. It will inspire you, energize you, help you to understand your value and purpose, and motivate you to become all that God created you to be. I believe this book will reach the hearts of young people all over the world and influence a generation for good.

—Stormie Omartian

Bestselling author of *The Power of a Praying* series, including
*The Power of a Praying Wife, The Power of a Praying Woman, The Power of a
Praying Parent, The Power of a Praying Teen,* and *The Power of a Praying Life*
(18 million books sold worldwide)

1

DIAGNOSIS

C ut!" the director called out to us on stage. Stopped in the middle of our "fight scene," my friend Brooke and I broke out of our characters and began to compose ourselves, picking off food that we had flung on each other during the scripted fight.

We were practicing for a community show based on Helen Keller's life. I was ten and Brooke was in her twenties…which made me Helen Keller and her Annie Sullivan, the teacher. This role was unlike any other I had *ever* taken on, as my primary goal was to believably play a deaf and blind girl.

Together, we worked for hours upon hours to get down the blind walk, brash grunts, and wild temper tantrums that were all a part of the story. Poor Brooke probably had bruises from the way I was instructed to flail about, and even hit and wrestle her in some scenes!

Gathering our things and collecting the director's notes after a long rehearsal, we were finally done for the night and it was time to head home. After the wildness of that food fight scene, I was convinced I'd gotten my workout for the night! My body had endured a few battle wounds itself from all of the crazy choreography. I looked forward to chilling for the rest of the night and secretly hoped I could talk my mom into taking me out for ice cream with some of the cast members. Dairy Queen wasn't too far from the theater and had become a popular spot for our post-rehearsal get-togethers. Besides, after all that food throwing I was ready for a Reese's Blizzard! I schemed the perfect way to convince Mom as I shuffled alongside her out to our car. But before I could get a word out she asked, "Paige, dear, what's wrong? Did you get a little too into your scene today?"

Completely distracted by my one-track-ice-cream mind, I gave her a confused look. "What do you mean?"

"I don't know..." She trailed off, then carried on. "It just looks like you're limping a little bit. I want to make sure you don't overdo it."

Hmm. My right leg has been kinda sore today, I thought...but with all the other bruises I probably had, I really didn't think much of it. "I'm sure it'll be gone by tomorrow," I reasoned. "Do you think we can go with the group to get ice cream?"

My mom laughed. She knew how my mind worked. "Not tonight, Paige. I think we should just get you home. It's been a long day."

Growing Pains

As time went on and I continued to rehearse for the play, take jazz, tap dance, and acting classes, and play sports with my homeschool group, the pain didn't go away. Instead of occasional discomfort or a barely-there limp, the pain became constant. When we went to the doctor, I was assured these "growing pains" would eventually stop. I've always been short, so hearing that it was growing pains was *such* awesome news! I couldn't wait to grow, and if it cost me a few leg aches I figured I could tough it out.

But the pain got worse.

Some nights, the part of my right leg under my knee would swell and turn red. The throbbing got so bad it kept me up for hours in tears. My older sister Kali, whose room was right next to mine, heard my moans in the night and came to comfort me. One night when she was hugging me, she told me she could feel my ribs and wondered if I was losing weight. I didn't seem to recall not having an appetite or looking any different than I normally did...but then again, I was ten, and didn't really worry about the pounds I was losing or gaining! All I knew was this pain *hurt*, I wasn't growing, and it wasn't going away.

My parents took me to several different doctors who ordered all kinds of X-rays—over and over and over again. They showed nothing. At that point, I started to figure either I was crazy or the doctors were! As it grew increasingly difficult to walk, I was given a straight brace to mobilize my leg. Every time the doctors tried to ask me what it felt like, I had a hard time describing what kind of "hurt" it was. The best insight I could give them was that it felt something like a pinched nerve. I didn't even know what a pinched nerve felt like, but it was the only description I could think of.

On one of the many discouraging days, after we'd come home with no new answers, I blurted out the words, "Mom…what if it's cancer?" Immediately, my family snapped their heads around as if I had just said, "I *am* cancer," and hushed my ridiculous thought.

A few weeks later the doctors suggested an MRI with the hope it would show something the X-rays didn't. I wasn't too happy about that idea, since the procedure involved a needle (of which I've never been too fond). Ultimately, my parents convinced me to have the procedure done so we could just get to the bottom of this mystery situation.

Several days after my MRI we met with the doctor so he could interpret my scans. I hobbled into his office in my leg brace, a parent on either side, to take a look at what they'd found. After seeing so many normal X-rays, I was shocked when the doctor explained that they had found a small mass just below my right knee. They said they were 99 percent sure it was a bone infection, but they would have to do a biopsy just to be certain.

Phew. So I wasn't going crazy after all! But what on earth did this mean? I heard the words *hospital* and *surgery*…at least, those were the words I knew. I remember thinking, *Man, I have to get surgery! That's going to stink. I'll miss dance, my friends…ugh. I did not sign up for this.*

But there was still that one percent chance it wasn't a bone infection. I didn't realize that it could be serious until we got in the car and my dad began calling my sisters and brothers. When I got home that afternoon, my family sat with me, cried, and held me as if I were about to be gone. I remember telling them I wasn't gone, and that I'd be fine. But *they* knew what that one-percent possibility could mean.

A Whole New World

The date of the biopsy came. I checked into the hospital the evening before my surgery. I didn't remember being in a hospital before, and had certainly never gone there to stay and have a surgery. As we walked in, I had a bone-chilling feeling I was entering into some sort of surreal world I wouldn't soon escape—a world that would be dark and isolated. This feeling terrified me, and with every step I took understanding started to hit me.

As we were shown the way into what became my room, we put our things down and breathed in the sterile air. In case I wasn't uncomfortable enough, they made me change into a hospital gown to begin some of the procedures. One of the first things they did was give me an IV. Everything in my heart was screaming, *Run for the hills, Paige! Get out while you still can!* And believe me, I wanted to. But there was no turning back now.

Some sweet friends and family had given me goodie bags to take to the hospital, equipped with CDs, games, stuffed animals—anything that might bring comfort or a smile. I felt incredibly thankful for those distractions, as I was desperate to get my mind off what was happening. Once connected to the IV and hooked up to the machines, I knew it wouldn't be long until surgery. Answers to months of mystery were only a few hours away.

The sound of machines and beeping woke me from a groggy sleep as I attempted to peel apart my eyelids. *Why is it so hard to open my eyes?* I finally managed to open them, only to find some lady I had never seen before coming into focus. "Well, hello dear," she said. "Looks like you're just starting to come to. Would you like me to call your parents?"

I guess I nodded my head or did something that got the message across, because I was quickly wheeled to the room where my family waited. The anesthesia had me so drugged I couldn't stay awake for more than a few minutes, but I was relieved to be out of surgery and have my family nearby.

The next time I woke, it was to an abrupt voice. Its owner was one of the hospital's physical therapists with a mission to get me up out of bed and walking on my crutches—only hours after my surgery, mind you! Still completely woozy from the drugs and in pain from the fresh surgery, it's safe to say I wasn't exactly the happiest camper. The therapist barked orders for me to stand up straight using my crutches and to take several steps down the hall. She was relentless until I performed her demands. Finally, after what seemed like boot camp on morphine, she released me back to my bed where I fell into a deep sleep.

This is where things get dark and blurry. I half remember eventually moving to another room, where days later several doctors and people I had never seen before gathered with my parents. We were finally given our long-awaited answer. Somewhere in that conversation, they explained that the mass they had been near-certain was a bone infection was actually a tumor. It was called Ewings Sarcoma.

I had cancer.

2
UPSIDE-DOWN WORLD

A soft knocking on the door woke me as a nurse peeked her head into my hospital room. "Paige," she said, smiling, "you've got some visitors! Can they come in?"

I nodded my groggy head as I readjusted my sore body. The Mac-Kenzies walked in. Kristin, their daughter, was one of my best friends and had the most beautiful head of blonde spiral curls I've ever seen!

"How are you feeling?" Mrs. MacKenzie asked.

"Okay, thanks," I managed. I had just had surgery a day before their visit to put a Broviac line into my chest, which acted as a permanent IV. This contraption would be necessary for the chemotherapy treatments that would begin in a few days.

"We brought you a few crafts and things to keep you busy!" Kristin said brightly as she handed them to me. "Your birthday's coming up. Did I hear your dad say you were thinking about having a party at your place?"

My mom, who sat over on her rollaway bed, took over the answer to this question. "Well, we're certainly hoping! The doctors want Paige to start chemo as soon as the Broviac heals up enough, which should be within the next day."

Chemo. Broviac. What were these words? And *Oncolo…uh, Oncology Unit?* This was apparently the section of the hospital where the doctors had moved me. Everything felt so foreign. I welcomed the sight of the MacKenzies. They were familiar, and at the moment, that was exactly what I needed.

Falling Out, Falling Apart

As I felt a little better later that day, my mom rolled me in a wheelchair from my room to the nurse's station. What an adventure! (It seriously was. After being cooped up in a room for days on end, you'd think so too!) One of the nurses asked me to play cards with her, so I wheeled up to the counter as she set up the deck.

I looked around the unit and counted seven rooms surrounding me. Each looked occupied, and I wondered who was in them. My nurse, Ann-Marie, dealt the cards and explained the game Spit. Suddenly distracted, my eyes moved to an opening door. I watched curiously to see who would emerge.

An IV pole with several different-colored bags of liquid hanging from it slowly wheeled out, pushed by a young girl attached to it by all sorts of tubes. Every step she took seemed to cost her a tremendous amount of effort as she dragged the pole by her side. I smiled when she looked at me, but I couldn't help but stare. She was the first patient I'd seen in this special seven-roomed unit. What terrified and fascinated me the most was something I didn't understand at all. She was *bald!* Why on earth was that? I convinced myself that it was just *her* condition.

Returning my attention to the cards, I shook off my thoughts and tried to jump into the game. Regardless of whether I was sick or not, this nurse was going down!

I quickly learned that any independence I'd previously enjoyed was now practically lost. Granted, I was only ten years old, but even the little freedom I'd had wasn't an option anymore. I couldn't get dressed, get out of bed, get food, or take a shower without help…and I *hated* it.

The Broviac installed in my right side could not get wet, which kept me from taking a shower. Sponge baths were the best option, so I took what I could get. My nurse and mom creatively washed my long, blonde hair in a bucket they secured on the bed. After we wrapped my sopping hair in a towel and cleaned up the wet mess, my nurse, Patti, sat down on my bed while my mom stood close by. Patti laid out what looked like a scrapbook and opened up its pages in front of me. I don't recall all that was said in that moment, but I do remember seeing pictures of kids who looked just like the girl I'd seen wheeling her pole out of the room. All the kids were *bald*.

Patti's words confirmed the panic that bubbled up inside me. That was about to be me. The chemo I would get the next day and for the next long while would make all of my hair fall out. Flipping through the pages, she showed me kids who had chosen to wear wigs that resembled the hair they used to have. She told me how wigs nowadays are so believable you can't even tell someone's wearing one!

But I could.

My mom came to my side and started rubbing my back. "I was thinking maybe you could get your hair cut. You know, cut at your chin like a bob."

I looked up at her with a clearly disturbed expression on my face.

"Paige, it will be easier to handle shorter hair falling out than the long hair you have now. Patti really thinks that would be the best thing."

The best thing? I'll tell you what would be the best thing! Ripping off these tubes, throwing my crutches out the window, and hightailing it out of here! What is happening *to me?*

But they were right. Cutting my hair *was* the best thing. Sure enough, every morning I found more and more strands on my pillowcase. Every time I ran my fingers through my hair they came away gripping a new handful. It only took the slightest tug, and the golden strands were taken from me.

As I watched my hair fall out, it felt like a metaphor for the rest of my life. *Everything* was falling out and falling apart…or so it seemed.

The Poison

The chemotherapy treatments were poisonous. I had only had two rounds out of fourteen, but it was more than enough to experience its painful and sickening side effects. I received a few different kinds of chemo. Some treatments were administered over five days and others over three days. Each of them caused different reactions. The effects were extreme: profound nausea, acid reflux, vomiting, raging bone pain, sensitivity to smell, loss of energy, weakened immune system, loss of red blood cells, skin peeling, shattering migraines, bruising, fevers, stomach cramps, and loss of appetite. These only name a few.

When the nurses pumped the poison through my Broviac IV, they wore extensive covering gear that looked like it was made for outer space travel! My parents cringed at the irony. Every inch of the nurses' bodies were sealed to protect them from the chemo fluids they were pumping *directly* into me.

I wasn't well enough to go home for more than a day or two, so the hospital became my new home. I'd be dismissed after days of receiving the chemo, only to come right back to the unit because of a spiking fever and other brutal side effects. The goal after each chemo treatment was merely to get me well enough to receive the next one. While the chemo certainly killed the cancer, it killed everything else along with it. That was the problem.

Blood cells and all kinds of other essential cells were wiped out with every treatment. Blood and platelet transfusions became a common part of my recovery. I had never received a bag of blood before, and the thought of it *freaked* me out! After the transfusion, I'd find myself with weird cravings for foods I had never wanted before. Apparently that happens sometimes when you get someone else's blood!

I lost weight rapidly, and every day it seemed the nutritionist visited and told me I was an inch away from being put on a feeding tube if I didn't start keeping my food down. My mom frantically tried to find *anything* that I would eat. She told me several years later that she knew if the doctors had inserted a feeding tube in me, a part of my spirit would have given up. She was desperate. And so was I.

Sure enough, we found a miracle in the form of a protein drink called Ensure. Every chance I could, I drank all that I could keep down, sip by tiny sip. It was just enough to sustain me and to keep the nutritionist from ordering the dreaded tube.

Each day was a struggle. Every moment a fight. Not only to keep my body going, but to keep my spirit alive.

Why Me?

When reality finally sank in, my naivety and shock wore off. It was as if one day I'd been a perfectly healthy little girl, and the next day I woke up in a cancer ward, bald and in a wheelchair. The mirror showed an image that wasn't myself, and it scared me. This frail person looked like a skeleton…a pale and bald one, emptied of any trace of the girl it once held.

My life in homeschool and the Theater Arts Center became a distant fantasy that seemed far too good to have ever happened. My friends were shaken too. One day I was just one of them, and the next—well…you know.

It surprised me to see who stood by my side during that time and who backed away, uncertain how to respond or what to say. I'll never forget one conversation with a friend who told me that I was "so lucky" to have cancer because I didn't have to go to school. She poured out her woes of awful teachers, too much homework, and how pathetically dramatic her classmates could be. While I tried to sympathize with the crumb of compassion I had left, my insides exploded. Had she really just said I was *lucky* to have cancer? Didn't she know I would have given anything to be able to go to school and live a normal life like her for even a day? That I would rather have a thousand math exams than a single round of chemo?

There was too much to say. I couldn't even speak.

My defenses were down around my mom, and when we were alone together I would let out my pain and anger. She was always with me, so she saw it all. One day when she was helping me bathe I remember hot tears streaming down my face as I asked her over and over again, "Why? Why is this happening to me? What did I do to deserve this?" I sobbed. I had never felt a pain so deep. I could only reason that God

was punishing me and had purposefully turned everything against me…
but I didn't know why.

I told my mom that I wished some of the kids I knew could have
cancer for a day—*just* a day. That would be enough. Enough for them
to realize the absolute bliss and beauty of the lives they had.

But honestly, I can't blame them. Because until cancer, I didn't
appreciate what I had either.

Face to Face with Death

One of my friends in the hospital was Allyse. She was a couple of
years older than me and had the same type of cancer that I did—except
this was her second time. After it had gone away the cancer had come
back in her lungs, only with more vengeance than before. Though my
family became good friends with her mom, I rarely saw Allyse because
she stayed in her room. She was always too sick, too tired, or not in the
mood to socialize. While I did understand the "too sick" part, I didn't
quite get her quietness. She seemed exceedingly sad, but at the time, I
didn't know why.

One rare night that I was actually able to be home, my dad got a
call from the hospital. Figuring it was just a standard check-in, I didn't
pay much attention…until my dad's tone changed, and I knew something was clearly wrong. He looked at me with devastated eyes and said,
"It's Allyse…She passed away tonight."

Horror gushed within me, followed by a surge of anger and confusion. I left the room and crutched my way up the stairs. I called a friend,
needing to pour out my emotions because they wouldn't stay bottled in.

I had never experienced death before, and certainly not from something that *I* had. It was all too real. *Much* too real. I couldn't wrap my
mind around the fact that one minute she was there, fighting like all of
us cancer kids, and the next it was over. How can that happen? Who
decides that it's her end?

I hung up the phone because I wanted an answer.

I took the journal beside my bed and scribbled out thoughts and
words and things that wouldn't make any sense if anyone else were to
read them. Then I found a new page and filled it with words like poetry.

Words full of pain and confusion, but words guided to hope. As my pen scribbled on, I suddenly realized what I was creating. Through the flow of the words, there was a verse, a chorus, another verse, and a bridge that was easily but unintentionally marked out.

I read each word in my mind and a melody followed, as if it were attached to the words. I softly sang what I had written and felt an unexpected comfort. Grabbing a little recorder in my room, I sang through what became my first song. Part of the chorus rang out the words, "There's a reason for everything," and I decided *that* would be the title.

This was a defining moment for me. Not only did I awaken to the reality of my own frailty, but of God's purpose in it. Without even knowing why, I knew I could trust Him. I really had nothing to base this feeling on, except that He was speaking to me, assuring me of this, and comforting me. He wasn't a distant God who throws lightning bolts down on us when we do something wrong. He is present, and not only cares about what happens, but will see us through it. Countless people had said that, but I guess it's one of those things you have to experience for yourself. Slowly, I was. He was there...and I was beginning to believe it.

3
THE WISH, THE HOPE

I t was time. I had battled cancer for five months and was about to undergo surgery to replace the bone that the tumor had sieged in my leg. So much depended on this moment.

Only one family member was allowed to walk next to me while I was being wheeled to the surgery room, so my dad took my hand and reminded me of the verses we'd recited from Psalm 121 as we were led down the maze of halls. We finally came to a set of massive metal doors whose only purpose seemed to be to intimidate the people who walked through them. At that point, I was asked to say goodbye to my dad—no one but the patient and the hospital staff were allowed to proceed further. He kissed my forehead and comfortingly squeezed the stuffed dog I clung to. Then they rolled me on.

Growing more and more anxious with every inch I was wheeled, terror overtook me. Looking down at my leg, I felt my stomach jump painfully in my throat at the thought of them replacing my bone. It was the last time I would ever see my leg look normal, untouched by a scar. I wanted to leap off the rolling bed but was surrounded by scrubs and white coats that left no crack for escape.

Seeing no way out, I closed my eyes and locked a death grip on my poor little stuffed dog. I replayed those verses my dad had recited over and over again. "My help comes from the LORD, the Maker of heaven and earth. He will not let your foot slip—he who watches over you will not slumber…the LORD is your shade at your right hand…The LORD will keep you from all harm."

As I shut out the terrifying world around me, I was brought into a strange presence that I had never felt before. It was as if Jesus Himself was truly there, holding me while they wheeled me in. Not in a clingy, over-protective way, but in a strong, safe, and all-knowing way. One that enveloped me in love and the sweetest peace I had ever known.

In this dark and desperate moment, I had the most intimate encounter with Jesus of my life. He was *real*. He was *there*. Jesus Himself was carrying me into that surgery room. I was precious to Him and every breath I took mattered. I knew it more than I ever had.

This day marked a change in my battle. Suddenly I wasn't fighting "God's scheme against me"—I was walking through the valley of the shadow of death, with my Savior lovingly holding my hand.

Surviving by Laughter

Though my perspective on the journey changed, getting through each day was still a struggle. It required faith, endurance, strong will, and laughter. Yes…*laughter*. There's humor in almost anything if you look for it.

Even in being bald.

After losing my hair I had a few wisps left, and at times I'd style those little strands into some sort of hairdo. For my old man impersonation, I combed the strands over to one side and hobbled over my crutch like a cane. For my Elvis impersonation, I gathered it all toward the front in a swirl and gave that crooked-lipped, "Thank yah very much." I could get everyone laughing with that one.

One of my favorite moments, however, was a genius prank that one of my nurses and I pulled. Getting an unused urine specimen cup and filling it with apple juice, we then crumbled little pieces of chocolate into it. Calling my other nurse in to give her the "specimen," she came and took it carefully as her eyes grew visibly disturbed. Clearing her throat she said, "Paige…this looks a little strange—is there something floating in there?!" Trying not to burst out laughing, I took the cup from her, pretending to be concerned, and examined it myself. "Oh! What is *that?*" I asked. As I began to unscrew the lid, I put my nose to the edge and sniffed it. Mumbling something about testing it, I brought the cup up to my lips to take a sip. Right then, Nurse Maria screamed at the top of her lungs, grabbing my arms to stop me from the horrid deed. I couldn't hold it any longer, and laughter *burst* from my lungs. Ginny, the other nurse I had plotted with, practically fell out of the bathroom she was hiding in. Roaring with laughter, we couldn't believe the perfection of the prank that we had just carried out! We were *good.*

I developed a reputation around the hospital as the prankster, and all kinds of other fun ideas began to flow. My little apple juice stunt had certainly made its way around and everyone knew to watch their back when it came to me. Even my dad wasn't safe. I would load up extra syringes with water to squirt him at the most unsuspecting moments.

It was one of the ways we kept our spirits alive. After all, each day I wanted to do more than just survive.

The Visitor

On one seemingly typical day in December, a bearded man walked into my hospital room with a guitar in his hands. His name was Woody, and he spent his days traveling from room to room in hospitals to play music for the kids being treated there. It was Christmastime when he came to visit me, and after playing a few songs to lift my spirits, he asked if I would be interested in singing a Christmas song with him. I hesitated because I hadn't sung in so long and didn't know what sounds would come out, but with the encouragement of my mom and sister Jenna, I agreed. I chose the song "Mary Did You Know?" and sang as he played along on the guitar. It felt so good to sing again. I was relieved that I still could!

After we finished the song, he looked at me and shared his surprise at my singing ability. He had a little digital recorder with him and asked if he could record me singing the song. We ended up creating a makeshift recording studio, right there in my hospital room, and recorded two Christmas songs.

Woody took our recordings to his home studio and had his friend Webb add piano. Woody then put the songs onto a CD and sent it out to me. On Christmas Eve, I gave the CD to my unsuspecting dad as a gift. Dad made *hundreds* of copies (as you can imagine a dad doing) and we gave them as a thank-you gift to everyone who had supported me with prayers and encouragement.

The response to the recording was astounding. We received countless notes saying what an inspiration this CD had been as people listened to it, knowing the difficulties I was going through. At a point when I thought cancer had taken everything, this little CD showed me that it hadn't. I still had something left to give.

My Wish

I wheeled myself in front of the mirror at my house and slipped on a newly purchased pink wig. It was *awesome*. My parents bought a few wigs after my hair fell out to try and resemble how I had looked before chemo. The other wigs were blonde like my original hair color, only in different styles and lengths, just for fun. Though I did like having hair to wear, I found myself mostly gravitating toward hats and bandanas. They were a million times more comfortable than wigs! The pink wig was really cool, though. I knew my parents would never let me dye my real hair pink so I figured the wig was the closest I would get to a wild hairdo.

The doorbell rang and I quickly snatched the wig off of my head and replaced it with a bandana. Volunteers from the Make-A-Wish Foundation were coming over, and I figured a pink wig might be a little much for our first introduction. The volunteers had scheduled a time to come to my house and talk with me about a wish that their organization would like to provide for me. The Make-A-Wish Foundation grants wishes to kids who suffer from life-threatening illnesses—giving them the chance to do whatever they can dream up. I had heard some of my hospital friends talk about their wishes. Some went to Disney World with their family, met their favorite bands, or went on a shopping spree. I was bubbling with excitement at the thought of having a wish of my own.

The Make-A-Wish volunteers came in and sat down with my parents and me, sharing the story of their foundation and explaining what a wish could consist of. Ultimately, our conversation came down to one mind-blowing question: "If you could do anything in the world, what would it be?"

A quietness settled in the room. *I have no idea!*

I blurted out a few things that came to mind, such as meeting Hilary Duff from *Lizzie McGuire* (I used to watch that show in the hospital a lot), or meeting a couple of my favorite Christian singers. But somehow I knew that I wasn't dreaming big enough...

It wasn't until later that my parents and I realized this could be an opportunity to do something far greater. With all of the feedback coming in from my little hospital recording, we wondered about making a real, professional CD—upgrading from my hospital "recording session."

So there it was. I wished to go to Nashville, Tennessee from my home in Pennsylvania and record a professional CD. I held my breath as I told my wish granters my idea, as, at the time, this wasn't the typical wish kids asked for. Fortunately, they didn't laugh or tell me to choose something else. They just started planning.

Finally, in June 2003, my wish was ready to be fulfilled. By this point, I had had fourteen rounds of chemotherapy and a major bone replacement surgery on my leg. I was pronounced cancer-free in 2002, and had just begun to get back on my feet and reclaim my life. This wish was the perfect opportunity to unlock dreams and hope that had been buried by my illness and time in the hospital.

On the day my parents and I left for my wish trip, we were picked up in a limousine and taken to the airport to fly to Music City itself—Nashville! There I would have two full days in a professional recording studio, get to sightsee, go to the Grand Ole Opry, and shop. I couldn't wait!

The two days that I spent in the recording studio were two of the most incredible days I had ever experienced. I got to sit amongst top-notch industry professionals who worked with the artists that I listened to and loved. I had my own producer, engineer, musicians, backup singers…the whole works!

Time only allowed us to record two songs, so we did one per day (each 13-hour days!). I chose the Twila Paris songs "The Warrior Is a Child" and "Lamb of God." Both were moving, inspirational ballads which the producer and band arranged beautifully.

While I was slightly intimidated to be singing in front of such seasoned professionals in a real recording studio, they made me feel at home and put me at ease. They treated me just like one of them.

Chance, one of the backup singers, even entered the vocal booth at one point to give me advice I've treasured ever since. He said to imagine the person who would hear the song, and sing as though they were the only person listening and they desperately needed to know the Lord. I needed to convey to them the hope of the lyrics. This precious and priceless advice reminded me of what my goal in singing was all about.

I Never Could Have Dreamed…

After I returned from my wish trip, we had the CDs packaged and began to give them out. The response blew us away.

As people heard this CD, a ministry unfolded for me that I never could have dreamed. A domino effect of opportunities came tumbling my way as I was asked to share my songs and story all over the country. At not quite 14 years old I was invited to sing and speak at black-tie corporate events, fundraisers, radio and TV programs, schools, and churches. One of the coolest parts was getting to fly under the radar and talk about the Lord in places where you normally couldn't talk about God! All I had to do was pull out the cancer card…and people suddenly became more accepting.

In 2005, I received the surprise of my life when Bath & Body Works asked to include me in their Christmas CD that featured celebrities like Jessica Simpson, Stevie Wonder, Martina McBride, and many more. This CD was set up to benefit the Make-A-Wish Foundation, and they wanted me to be the ambassador for it.

Once again I was sent down to Nashville to record five Christmas songs. There were three CDs in the package, two with the celebrities' songs and one with mine. My CD included not only songs, but also a video interview in which I talked about my wish and shared my testimony.

As if that weren't incredible enough, Bath & Body Works sent me on a nationwide media tour to sing and be interviewed on TV and radio shows. Two of these programs were NBC's *Today Show* and *Extra!*

I was officially in disbelief.

What had happened? It was as if God had opened the floodgates after healing me of cancer. I was overwhelmed with blessings, and absolutely in awe of where He had brought me.

His Plan...All Along

So many people told me that God had a plan when I was in the midst of suffering. But at the time, it sounded like nothing more than a polite cliché.

Now, on the other side of it, I see that they were right. He did have a plan, and He never left me hanging...not even once. He was using my pain to deepen my faith, grow me, and teach me invaluable lessons. I see that now with a more mature hindsight. He opened my heart to realities that I never would have known existed without the battle I was intended to fight.

Romans 8:28 says, "And we know that in all things God works for the good of those who love him, who have been called according to his purpose."

This is my life verse, because I have found it to be unmistakably true. God has taken the worst thing in my life and brought about the best things. He took my pain and exchanged it for purpose.

Honestly, even if I could go back and take away my battle with cancer, as horrible as it was, I wouldn't. God has used that circumstance to unleash my purpose and instill a passion in me that I'm devoted to living out.

I wrote a song called "The Story Song" with these lyrics:

No one's spared to just keep silent,
No one's saved to just keep still.
So what's your story?
And will you live it out?

This is my story, but that's not what this book is about. Each one of us has a story—a purpose, a calling, and a charge to live it out.

So what's *your* story? The journey starts now.

4

YOUNG AND
HOPELESS

The bell rang and I leaped from the desk and headed to my locker to enjoy our school's ten-minute break. I hurried down the hall to stop in the bathroom, where I found girls from my class primping in front of the mirror. This was the usual time to fix hair or reapply lip gloss. The bathroom was loaded and you practically needed a VIP invite to get in.

A mix of chatter, laughter, and moans arose from the "primpers" according to the mood of their day. I leaned in to sneak a spot at the counter when one girl shrieked, *"I hate my hair!"* She combed it furiously with her fingers and then flung her hands into the air in exasperation. "I can't get it to do anything today! I wish I could shave it all off!"

My emotions screeched to a halt and smashed into the words I'd just heard.

Shave it all off? Girl, are you nuts? I just was bald, and I can guarantee you wouldn't want to try that!

I gathered my things and slipped out the door while the other girls sympathized about how frustrating bad hair days can be.

Welcome to seventh grade. After a year of being holed up in the hospital and surrounded by cancer patients, I certainly wasn't in Kansas anymore. My treatments ended in April, and I decided I wanted to try going to school in the fall. My hair was about an inch long, but I didn't care—I was just happy to have some! I was still learning how to walk again after my major leg surgery, but I did everything I could to mask the limp.

Looking back now, I see the risk that I took in even going to school that year. While I thought this was a step toward once again being normal, I definitely didn't fit that definition. Not with how I looked, at least…and as I came to find out, not with how I thought either.

I had just survived a world where each day was not only precious, but fought for. A world where nothing was taken for granted. A world where you were simply thankful to be alive.

Then, in my quest to be normal again, I stepped into seventh grade. *Normal* among my peers meant feeling invincible. *Normal* was blowing off anything important just to mess around and do what we wanted. *Normal* was wasting our lives.

I had stepped into a complete culture shock, and frankly, the incident in the girls' bathroom was the least of the surprises.

The Norm

During this time of adjustment, I wrote a note that I put on my MySpace page (back when MySpace was the "it" site). I want to share a portion of that note as it gives a window into what I was experiencing.

> I can't sleep, and it's after two in the morning…so I go online to look at some friends' pages that I haven't seen in a while and just chill. The sad thing is, I'm finding more and more people are slipping away from who I thought they were, and who they profess to be. Suddenly, alcohol, drugs, sex, and swearing have become their pastimes, yet in some twisted way it's woven in with this "love of God" and "Christian walk" that they try to wear on Sundays and youth group nights. This world is messed up. Most of what's good has been tainted, and most of what's bad has become the norm.

Honestly, sometimes I get tired of trying to do the right thing and trying so hard to do what God wants. Sometimes I just want to be like everyone else—a normal teen. I want to live a little, take some risks, be dangerous, live on the edge, get crazy. But you know some of the statistics for normal teens? Seven out of ten teens have had sex by the time they're nineteen. An immense number of teens are cutting themselves on a regular basis, and the third leading cause of death in teens is suicide. So I want to be "normal," huh?

Maybe it's because we've gotten so numb to all this that we don't really care. Maybe we've been bombarded by so much that we hardly know what's right and wrong anymore. Maybe it's because we've let people push us around so often that we've forgotten who we are and what we even want in life.

Whatever it is, is that how you want to live? Everyone is just dying to be accepted, dying for something real, dying for someone to love them. But everyone is dying in this way of living...

So I made up my mind. The "norm" I so desperately wanted to fit into was the very thing I ran from. This norm is played out in more ways than just sex, drugs, and alcohol. It's a mindset, not merely an action. This mindset wears the face of apathy, the hands of rebellion, and the heart of worthlessness. It eagerly accepts the "lost cause" title that society has crowned on us, and we blindly sing its anthem.

The Face of Apathy

On the surface, apathy looks very different on each person. Let's check out four different ways that apathy can show up in people.

1. **The Needer:** This person has a hard time being alone. They don't have any particular goals for themselves, which often leads them to depend on other people for entertainment, plans, and fulfillment. The Needer has very self-centered

tendencies and can be known as a kind of leech, constantly sucking the life from others because they are too apathetic to get a life themselves.

2. **The Pleaser:** This one is especially common as the person is driven by a desire to be liked and accepted. Many times, unknowingly, they will sacrifice their personal values or beliefs to fit in with a trendy opinion. Their apathy comes in the form of succumbing to the views of others because they don't seek out or stand up for the truth themselves.

3. **The Neither:** This person doesn't care either way. No rules, no guidelines, no suggestions or demands apply to them because they've removed themselves entirely from the game. They prefer to sit out or not even try, because they believe there is no reason. Their apathy is in their complete lack of motivation and the idea that "it won't matter anyway."

4. **The Ring Leader:** This is the person who seeks attention, and doesn't care what they have to do to get it. "The Ring Leader" always seems to be sucking others into their latest whim and deliberately living on the edge of rebellion. They thrive off of the attention and rush of being wild and are the first to dismiss the disapproval of others. Their apathy lies within their neglect to realize the impact of their life and the preciousness of their reputation.

If you're like me, you can easily envision at least one person you know for each of those categories. But watch out—it's always easier to identify these attitudes in someone else. The question is—are *you* one? Is there anything in those classifications that reflects your tendencies, personality, or outlook on life?

Personally, between those four options I tend toward *The Pleaser*. Granted, this doesn't describe me completely, but I do struggle with people-pleasing at times and have to really force myself to seek the truth and stand on it at all costs—even when it makes me unpopular.

We can only begin this awakening journey when we hold up a

mirror to see our true selves. We must know where we are starting before we embark on the journey.

The Hands of Rebellion

There's something deep inside most of us young people that likes rebellion. We like our music loud, our parties hard, and our spirits free. To an extent, I believe this "wild heart" has always been a part of youth. It's the beauty of our innocence and passion to discover an uncharted world.

God warns us, however, against the part of our spirit that leads us into rebellion against Him. Second Timothy 2:22 says, "Flee the evil desires of youth and pursue righteousness, faith, love and peace, along with those who call on the Lord out of a pure heart."

While our hearts are prone to dance on the edge of the wild side, we were made to use our passion in a holy way. The fire in our hearts can either bring life or destroy our very being. With the help of a changing culture and advancements in media, our innocence has been replaced with unlimited access to an increasingly provocative world. Every kind of evil is at our fingertips—only one touch, click, or dial away.

Worse than the temptation, however, is the expectation we feel our culture placing on us to be rebellious, wild, and do stupid things. We have a stereotype hanging over our heads that says we're "just teenagers." Yet instead of feeling upset that we've been belittled, we seem to have bought into it. We use "well, we're just kids" as an excuse for a rebellious and careless attitude. I know I've used it.

You know why? Because it was easy. It was a cop-out. That excuse justified my irrational, defiant decisions and even sprinkled "blessing" on them because that's what the world expected. As much as I tried to convince myself that this mindset was normal and just the way things were, deep down I knew it was wrong. I knew I was meant for more than this condescending compromise.

Titles such as "rebel without a cause" have practically become our definition. The strange thing is, it wasn't always this way. In 1955 James Dean starred in a film with that very title—*Rebel Without a Cause*. This movie helped introduce a new kind of mentality in the young generation. It made history as it hit the theaters, emphasizing the restless, misunderstood, rebellious hearts of the youth—and depicted a tense generational gap between teens and their parents.

In past generations—prior to the glamorization of youth rebellion—young people were held to a much higher standard. They were expected to carry themselves in a respectable way, honor their elders, learn a trade, and do the work of an adult.

As Alex and Brett Harris pointed out in their book *Do Hard Things*, the word "teenager" didn't even exist until it was published in Reader's Digest in 1941.* The word "teenager" has robbed us of the "adult" in young adult. It now comes with the connotation of being troubled, aimless, wild, and even hopeless.

Heart of Worthlessness

There was a guy I knew in high school who used to get in trouble for everything. On the surface he had a rough exterior and didn't seem to be touched by anyone or anything. He would make the most inappropriate jokes, say the cruelest things, and push the limits at every opportunity. There was a time, though, when I saw his shell begin to crack. He had just gotten into his worst trouble yet and was about to be expelled from school. Something in his "unbreakable" exterior began to crumble and reveal a very different person from the one he had previously portrayed. For the first time, I saw in him a broken little boy. I saw someone who spent his life trying to impress people and convince them that he was a tough guy. I saw someone who wanted others to notice him and to believe for himself that he had worth.

Under the skin of even the fiercest rebel is the feeling of worthlessness. Most of us, no matter how thick our façade, struggle with this. We feel like a mess emotionally, physically, directionally...not to mention spiritually. But the strangest thing is that this walking mess mentality seems to be popular—even cool. As a young person, being

---

* Alex Harris and Brett Harris, *Do Hard Things: A Teenage Rebellion Against Low Expectations* (Colorado Springs: Multnomah, 2008).

messed up is portrayed as kind of edgy, mysterious, and attractive. It comes with the territory of being young, and gives us permission to have angst and attitude. Besides, all the celebrities are doing it!

This worthless, messy mindset sparks the idea that everyone is against us and that we have to fend for ourselves. Many feel like it's them against the world, that no one's going to come save them, so they've got to make it on their own. Have we buried ourselves so deep in our feeling of worthlessness that our only option is to hide in our mess and turn a cold shoulder to all else?

The Biggest Lie

Somewhere along the way we've gotten the message that we are of no value. We have been told that what we do doesn't matter—that we are insignificant, incapable, and unworthy.

That is the biggest lie.

Let me say it again, so you don't miss it. *That is the biggest lie.*

The truth is, every second matters.

God wants to rescue us from the degrading mindset the world has given us and exchange it for a purpose and value. I can feel the Lord saying, "Wake up, generation! I created you for more than this."

If you're tired of a mediocre life, it's because you weren't made for one. You were created for more.

First Timothy 4:12 says, "Don't let anyone look down on you because you are young, but set an example for the believers in speech, in conduct, in love, in faith and in purity." God went out of His way to address these "low expectations" on youth by specifically telling us to not let anyone expect less from us because of our age. You and I are to be leaders, to be examples of God to everyone around us.

We don't have to wait until our mid-life crisis to get things together. In fact, we can't. God is calling us now, at exactly the age we are, for a breathtaking purpose. We don't have time to be limited by age. What does a number have to do with it anyway?

This is a poem I wrote when I was 18 years old, out of frustration from the low expectations that I experienced because of my age.

I Am 18

I am what I am
Don't you make me to be
Anything less than the true heart of me.
If eighteen is a number,
Then what could it mean?
Does it limit my thoughts, my passions and dreams?
Take me out of your box,
I have no place there.
I'm too wild for that,
It wouldn't be fair.
If you say that you know me,
Then look me inside
And ask me the questions you think that I'll hide.
I'm perfectly willing to open your eyes,
Are you too scared to look into mine?
I'm more than the song you've forgotten to play,
I'm more than the words you can't seem to say.
If eighteen is a number,
Then why do you care?
Does it change who I am,
Or all that I've shared?
Don't you tell me the things you want me to be.
Who are you to say what you think you should see?
If I am what I am,
Then eighteen is my age.
But a number is not what defines me today.

ACTION CHALLENGE

Starting here, we are going to have an Action Challenge at the end of every chapter. This is designed to help you take what's discussed in each section and turn it into real, tangible change in your life.

1. Consider the ways that culture's low expectations for young people

have affected you. What norm have you accepted in your life that is not biblical? In what ways do you feel that God is calling you to be an example?

2. Write down 1 Timothy 4:12, either on a sticky note you post on your wall or a card you carry in your pocket. Let this be a constant reminder of *God's* expectation for you to be the man or woman He has called you to be.

3. Just for fun: How old would you be if you didn't know how old you were?

5

R U BORED?

I t's everywhere. It's the fastest growing disease among young people ages 13 to 25. This epidemic has infected family, friends…maybe even you. The cause is still under research, but it is confirmed to be incredibly contagious, and even deadly. Those who have suffered from the disease were unaware of its initial onslaught, but the devastation of the effects is unmistakable and leaves its victims desperate.

Before I tell you the name of this disease, let me share the story of a friend who suffered from it. Perhaps you'll recognize its symptoms.

John was a junior in high school, a fun and popular guy. Everyone seemed to like him. He was smooth…not only with the girls, but when it came to being cool with the guys too. He knew how to act around all different types of people. For the wild crowd, he was the life of the party. For the more conservative bunch, he was thoughtful and reserved.

I met John at a time when he seemed to really be searching for something more in life. We weren't great friends then, but he opened up to me regarding his walk with the Lord and shared that he knew he'd fallen away and needed to make things right. He was caught between two selves—one who knew no boundaries, and the other who longed for a greater purpose. I encouraged him in his soul-searching and challenged him to return to God. As I talked to him in the weeks that followed, he legitimately seemed to be seeking the Lord and taking steps to change. I felt excited for him and wanted to be as supportive as I could along the journey.

One day, I got a call from him that started out like most…but as his voice staggered on, I knew something was wrong.

I probed as gently as I could, and out gushed the story of the night before. With shame and regret in his voice, he told how he had been coaxed into smoking pot with his friends and had driven to a party completely high. Once he got to the party, he drank until he could hardly function, and the next thing he remembered was waking up in a random bed with a girl he didn't even know.

I swallowed awkwardly a few times as I tried to take it all in. What should I say to this? Where had this come from, and how could it have happened? I thought he had turned away from that lifestyle.

The question *How did this end up happening? What made you even start?* pounded over and over in my mind until I finally blurted it out.

His answer, however, was what astounded me most.

"I don't know, Paige. It was a Friday night and I was bored…it seemed like there was nothing better to do."

Nothing better to do.

Nothing better to do?

You're telling me that you ended up in that situation because you were *bored?*

That marked the hour that I knew there was a problem. A diagnosis had been born; a disease was taking over. It is called the Bored Epidemic.

The Bored Epidemic

Have you ever heard anyone say, or even said yourself, "I'm bored"?

My parents cured me at a young age. If they heard me utter that phrase, they quickly gave me some awful chore. That was probably the fastest lesson I learned! (Around the house at least.)

So we can put away the pointed finger because we've all said it. "I'm bored" has become one of the most common phrases our generation uses.

I see people write it all the time online. If I had a nickel for every "bored" status I see, I'd be filthy rich! Unfortunately, no one gives me nickels...

The phrase itself seems innocent enough, but these two words are way more than just a common phrase. They've become a lifestyle.

In our culture, we are constantly being entertained. We can fill every second with something that occupies our eyes, our ears, and our brains. Unlike previous generations, few of us had to entertain ourselves as children. Have you ever sat with a toddler to play? They may be fascinated with Legos one minute, but after 60 seconds they're completely uninterested and on to the next light-up plastic Fisher-Price distraction.

Our attention span has become like a toddler's. We live in a flashy 15-second clip culture that has trained our minds to get bored after a short period of time. This kind of environment is where our boredom has taken root and grown into a lifestyle of seeking distractions, quick fixes, and ways to pass the time.

Perhaps for some of you, the story I shared about my friend John seems more extreme than you can relate to. Make no mistake: the everyday boredom we experience, even in small ways, can be just as devastating.

To see how this applies to us on a daily level, take a little "bored evaluation" and see if you've caught the symptoms. Put a check mark by each statement that sounds like you. (Be honest! No one's going to hunt you down!)

Bored Evaluation

- When I don't have school, work, or something else going on, I get bored.

- I sit at home, randomly surfing the computer or TV when I don't know what else to do.

- I have to find someone to hang out with when nothing else is going on.

- I don't care what I do with my friends, as long as I'm not at home alone on a Friday night.

- When I'm alone, I have no idea what to do with my time.
- I find myself bored very often…at least several times a week.
- I hate when my schedule slows down, because I don't know what to do.
- At times I've done stupid stuff, all because I was initially bored.
- I don't have anything I particularly work on outside the things that are required (school, work, chores, etc.).
- I've posted statuses online saying I'm bored.
- I often find myself unmotivated and wishing I knew how to better use my time.
- Sometimes I get frustrated or feel bad about how bored I am.
- I end up wasting a lot of time when I'm bored.

How many did you end up checking? Were you surprised how many applied to you?

I recently surveyed some young people and asked why they think they get bored. This question received quite the array of responses, but the main ones were:

- Not knowing what to do with my time
- Not having a life
- Lack of really awesome things to do
- Apathy, lack of motivation

These reasons are very interesting to me, and we're actually going to cover each of them in this book. The truth is, I don't believe any of them are legit. If these reasons drive how we spend our days, we need to take another look at our perspective here on earth.

The Mist

Have you ever thought about the timespan of your life? How many years will you live? How much time will you have on this earth?

It's funny how time can seem to travel different speeds according to what we're experiencing. The last few weeks before school lets out inch along like eternity, yet summer flies by! And an embarrassing moment (we've all been there) can seem to last for hours, but a few hours of time spent with a loved one can feel like minutes.

Time is elusive, untouchable, and incomprehensible. Yet the one thing we can know for certain about it is this: it's not promised.

One of the most life-changing, eye-opening verses I ever read is James 4:14. "Why, you do not even know what will happen tomorrow. What is your life? You are a mist that appears for a little while and then vanishes."

The Message translation puts it a little more harshly: "You don't know the first thing about tomorrow. You're nothing but a wisp of fog, catching a brief bit of sun before disappearing."

Yikes. That's almost a slap in the face. Is our time on earth truly this fleeting? Sometimes I wonder…if we really lived like our lives were a mist, how different would our lives be? Songs like "Live Like You Were Dying" and movies such as *The Bucket List* share the reality of what one would do if they realized they were about to die. Once they caught the glimpse of reality, they had a whole list of things that they wished they had known or done sooner.

Several years after being healed of cancer, I walked the halls of the hospital for a routine checkup. Hospitals always bring back my old memories of feeling trapped. As I walked down the hall, I saw patients attached to tubes and IV poles, being wheeled in their hospital beds with scared, half-conscious faces, wondering what was happening to them.

I couldn't help but ask this: Why do we have to walk through the valley of the shadow of death before we realize our lives are so precious?

How many of these people, I wondered, find themselves in the hospital bed or on their death bed, mourning not because of the pain of needles, treatments, and surgeries, but at their wasted lives? Oh, what they would give to get it back and do things right. To live for something greater. To truly use their lives.

Reality Check

As young people, we have a tendency to think that we're not only invincible, but have all the time in the world to figure things out or make everything right in our lives. I'm 21 years old as I write this book, and it's a miracle that I'm still alive. You may be my age, younger, or older, and it's just as much a miracle that you are alive.

Every second that we have life is for a reason. If you're breathing, it means there is something left for you to do. Your life is not an accident. You have been handpicked and placed on this earth for a purpose. Your life was chosen. It's precious.

What really captured my attention during my time in the hospital was seeing so many kids who were extremely sick, fighting for the chance to live one more day, while other perfectly healthy friends were barely living theirs. This didn't make sense. How could one fight for their life, and the other throw it away?

Wake Up

We need to open our eyes.

If we complain of not having a life, we're not living it! If we feel we have nothing better to do, we have everything better to do! We've been sleepwalking in apathy, passive in our motivations, blinded to the incredible adventure that God wants to breathe into our lives. We have a mission, a role in a story that is bigger than ourselves, beyond what we could imagine.

The fact is, until world peace is a reality, no child goes to bed hungry, lives and families are unbroken, and every soul has heard the Gospel of Christ, there is no room for any one of us to be bored! God has handpicked each of us and positioned us in this time and in this place with a purpose to fulfill. Our life is precious—there's no time to sit around.

"Wake up from your sleep, climb out of your coffins; Christ will show you the light! So watch your step. Use your head. Make the most of every chance you get. These are desperate times!" (Ephesians 5:14-16 MSG).

Wake up! Rise from the dead! You're alive, but have you been living? Leave your old ways behind. Christ will guide you. He will inspire your steps.

The time has come for our generation to throw off the shackles of apathy, reclaim our value, and uncover our purpose. God is calling each one of us to something new and fresh that He wants to do in our lives. He longs to revive our soul and set our paths straight. He delights in unveiling our value in the most stunning, priceless way. He desires to awaken our soul.

Wake up. You don't have a second to waste.

ACTION CHALLENGE

1. Catch yourself anytime you're about to say the poisonous words, "I'm bored!" Remove the phrase from your vocabulary completely, and see what happens!

2. Make a list of some things you can do the next time you feel bored. Sometimes in the unmotivated moment it's hard to think of anything to do, but if you pull together some ideas ahead of time, you can refer to it in your time of need. Use this spare time to be creative, reconnect with friends, spend time with the Lord, or start a new project.

3. When a friend calls to hang out, have a purpose in getting together. That can be just getting together to talk or watch a movie, but be careful of those who just like to hang out because they have nothing better to do. Those kinds of friends need to get a life.

6

WHO, ME?

It was late one night and I was rustling around my room, frustrated, as I tried to finish my AP History homework. *Why on earth did I sign up for this class again?* I wondered.

My teacher, Mr. Cutsinger, was a wonderful man who sprinkled our 45-minute class periods with his off-the-wall, dry sense of humor. That course made me laugh and cry all at the same time. I had never seen so much homework! Papers to write every day, countless pages of reading...I was sure I had entered into AP History boot camp.

On the second day of class more than half of the students dropped out...and several days later I was wondering why I hadn't been one of them! But no, persistence and discipline were key. I didn't like the sound of dropping out of something, so (perhaps for stubborn reasons) I marched on!

This night, like many sleepless others, I plugged away at my homework and dreamed of being fast asleep, snuggled in my bed. I desperately wanted a break from the paper that I was writing, but I knew if I took a nap, I'd never regain consciousness. Yet my mind was spinning and my eyes were foggy so I threw on a jacket, headed down the stairs, and went outside.

The night was crisp and fresh. It felt good to be out of my room and in the freeing air. I paced around our patio, then through the grass and onto our driveway, where I decided to lay down on the pavement. As I stretched out with my face toward the sky, I was startled by the breathtaking view that consumed my eyes. Straight above me was a blanket of pure black sky with the most brilliant stars I'd ever seen. It was a perfectly clear night, and every star and visible planet burned with a radiance that lit up the darkness.

I was mesmerized. In a matter of seconds I was completely swept up in this gigantic display of the universe suspended above me. Suddenly the ground that I was laying on felt as though it were shrinking, and like I was getting smaller with it. I felt like Alice in *Alice in Wonderland* when she drank the potion and shrunk to the size of a mouse.

I had never felt so small.

As I laid there staring at this panorama, I couldn't help but feel ridiculous. How could I ever get so wrapped up in myself? I'm hardly a speck in this grand universe. I'm engulfed by only a glimpse of one of the numerous galaxies that God has created.

It was scary to be put in my place. I was humbled, finally understanding that I barely deserved the right to utter a word before such a huge and magnificent God. My mind flashed to an image I'd seen once, taken from far off in space. At first glance, it almost seemed like there was nothing even in the picture. I tried to brush away what I thought was a piece of lint on my computer screen until it hit me. That was the Earth. The camera had wandered out so far into space that it made Earth look like dust on my screen.

Thinking of that image and the splendor above me, I laid in my driveway in silence, hardly able to take it all in. I felt heavy with the awareness of my puny, seemingly insignificant existence.

And then I thought of Jesus.

With disbelief flooding through my body, I thought of Jesus on the cross and the fact that He came to this minuscule world to die for us. The Creator of the universe humbled Himself to come in human form, to be rejected, persecuted, humiliated, and murdered. For us?

In that moment, while I felt smaller than a speck, I was over-whelmed by the most incredible realization.

God loves me. *God* loves me. God loves *me*!

I had never felt so loved, so cho-sen, and cherished in my life.

The Least Likely

I often feel like David, the writer of many of the psalms, when he says, "When I consider your heav-ens, the work of your fingers, the moon and the stars, which you have set in place, what is mankind that you are mindful of them, human beings that you care for them?" (Psalm 8:3-4).

> Can you fathom the mysteries of God? Can you probe the limits of the Almighty? They are higher than the heavens above— what can you do? They are deeper than the depths below—what can you know? Their measure is longer than the earth and wider than the sea.
>
> —*JOB 11:7-9*

While it is true that we are small and insignificant, because of the image of God within us we are of greater worth than anything else in all creation. We have been bought at the highest price: the blood of Christ. Our lives are so valuable that He died just so we could live. "But God demonstrates his own love for us in this: While we were still sin-ners, Christ died for us" (Romans 5:8).

Can we even wrap our minds around that? He died for you. He died for me. Do we have any idea how unbelievably precious that makes us? Do we even accept that?

Deep down at our core, each one of us can feel unworthy of love, incapable of doing anything of worth or importance in this world. Many of us don't expect that God would want to use us, or that He even could! We reason that He only uses the "super spiritual"—the people who seem to have come out of the womb reciting Scripture, who always know the right and godly thing to do. We shake our heads when we hear that God wants to use us, thinking, *Ohhh no...He couldn't possibly mean me!*

But He does.

Just when you've convinced yourself that you are the last person on the planet that God would ever call to do something significant, rest assured: You are actually the perfect candidate.

In the beginning, God made the universe—the earth, stars and galaxies—from nothing. Once He created the ground, He took some dust from it and made a brilliantly complex human being. God's very nature is about taking nothing and turning it into something extraordinary. How much more will He do with us if we're willing? As the apostle Paul said, "God chose the foolish things of the world to shame the wise; God chose the weak things of the world to shame the strong. God chose the lowly things of this world and the despised things—and the things that are not—to nullify the things that are, so that no one may boast before Him" (1 Corinthians 1:27-29).

I don't know about you, but I find this pretty comforting. No matter how big a disaster you and I are in, there is hope! God doesn't cast us aside; He chooses us. God is calling each one of us by name for a specific purpose.

The only question is…are we responding?

The Call

Sometimes we think we need the booming voice of God to wake us in the night if we're going to be called to something. We hear pastors and missionaries talk about being "called into the ministry," but we wonder if that really applies to us. What does it mean to be called to something, anyway?

Think of your "calling" as being *called by name for a specific purpose.*

Scripture says, "His divine power has given us everything we need for a godly life through our knowledge of him who called us by his own glory and goodness. Through these he has given us his very great and precious promises" (2 Peter 1:3-4).

According to this verse, every single one of us is equipped with all we need to serve God…now. Right before us sits the purpose for which He has created us. He has called us to that purpose by His glory and goodness, and says that—in Him—we have everything necessary to fulfill it.

We can respond to this call in several ways:

1. Try to talk God out of it. I've totally done this! Sometimes when God has brought certain opportunities into my life—things that I knew He was asking me to do—I responded with a scroll of reasons why I wasn't the right person. I tried to convince Him that I was inadequate for the job and even offered suggestions of someone else who could do it better! Moses did the same thing when God called him go before Pharaoh and lead the Israelites out of Egypt. Moses trembled at the thought. He pleaded with God, saying that he was not a good speaker, and asked the Lord to send someone else to do it (Exodus 4:10,13).

2. Run! Believe it or not, there are many men and women who actually know deep down what they are called to, but are intentionally running in the opposite direction. A friend of mine, a youth pastor, shared the resentment he used to have toward his father's ministry. Though he felt he was ultimately being called to youth ministry, he did everything in his power to rebel against that calling. It wasn't until God brought his life to a screeching halt that he finally stopped running and submitted to his vocation. Now when you see him working with youth, it couldn't be any more obvious that youth ministry is what he was made for. (Please know that I'm in no way trying to suggest that you are called to the same thing that your parent was called to. Each path is completely unique. No one else has your specific calling!) The bottom line is, we need to be open to hear what God is calling us to…and be obedient to follow it. Check out the story of Jonah in the Bible! Remember where running from God landed him?

3. Accept. One of the most amazing stories of calling that I know is Mary's—Jesus's mother. This sweet young girl was engaged to be married when she was visited by an angel and told the craziest news anyone could ever hear. She

was going to have God's child! Any normal person would have probably had a meltdown or asked a million terrified, panicked, and doubtful questions. But Mary didn't. Her response was simple and sure: "I am the Lord's servant," she said. "May your word to me be fulfilled" (Luke 1:38).

How are you responding to God's calling on your life? Maybe you don't know what it is yet. Maybe deep down you know, but there's a fear that keeps you running from it. Maybe you're overwhelmed and you simply feel inadequate. Perhaps, like Mary, you have graciously and obediently accepted it, but you're unsure of what this means from here on out. Wherever you are…start there. Throw off every other person's expectation and know that the God of the universe has chosen you, has *called you by name for a purpose*. You may not know what it is yet, but He will not leave you hanging.

Mark's Story

Mark grew up in a Northeastern town in New Jersey. While he was a leader on his school's sports team, he didn't really feel that he had enough influence to be a leader outside of that sphere as well. As a kid, he carried around the sense that the world was too big and he was too small to make an impact. Though raised in a Christian home, his faith, he admitted, wasn't real to him. When he was 15, his mom was diagnosed with cancer and told that she only had a short amount of time left to live. What little faith Mark had was shaken. The desperate circumstance of his mom's condition brought him to a place where he could no longer rely on himself. There was nothing left to hold on to. He needed God.

Mark had always loved music, but during this struggle it developed into a passion. It gave him an outlet for his emotions. He took up playing the drums, and even though he still wasn't sure what he thought about church, his love for music drew him to play with the worship team. It was there that he met Tim, the new 24-year-old worship leader who had just joined the team and who ended up becoming an incredible mentor. Mark watched the way that Tim led worship and realized he was involved in something that affected, even changed people. Drawn to it, Mark secretly longed to have that kind of influence himself. As his own relationship with God was deepening, he developed a passion for worship and began to learn what true worship really meant—how it was not merely a song, but a way of life. Mark's passion ignited as he wrote songs and played with the worship team. He realized that this was a gifting, and an outlet for him to share things that connected him with others.

This was the start of uncovering a great calling. God used Mark's passion for music to carry him not only into a deeper relationship with Him, but also into His purpose. "I feel like the growth in my spiritual life has been directly intertwined with the discovery of my gifts," he shared. "And you see that all the time in the Bible. You read in Scripture how God specifically used people's gifts and life calling to bring them into a more intimate walk with Him."

When I asked Mark what his calling looks like and how he is living it out, he responded, "I feel called to build relationships with people who are searching," he responded. "I want the ability to work in their lives through and because of God—that together, we might know more of who He is."

Mark is currently living this calling out in a number of ways. God has opened doors for him to write songs with accomplished artists, perform as a musician, speak, and lead worship on platforms all over the country. Recently, he started a ministry called *Next* with a pastor friend. The ministry's vision was to gather people in the community, serving the lost and sharing Christ with them. They put together outreach events on the streets of some of the poorest and most dangerous areas in New Jersey, served at soup kitchens, ministered at AIDS walks, and even put together a Christmas Eve service for all the homeless in the surrounding area. This wasn't managed by an accomplished professional, but by a young guy fresh out of high school. A guy who grew up thinking he was too small to make a

> "You are my witnesses," declares the LORD, "and my servant whom I have chosen."
>
> —ISAIAH 43:10

difference. This is Mark. The same guy who now leads homeless people to Christ, inspires jailed convicts to a new life, and leads crowds into passionate worship before God.

This is what God does. He trades our puny worthlessness for something priceless, intricately crafted, and powerfully significant.

He answers our vulnerable question with His knowing, gracious words…

"Yes, you."

ACTION CHALLENGE

1. Go to www.paigeomartian.com and check out the video under the Chapter 6 tab. See for yourself what a speck the earth really is.

2. Go outside on a clear night and find a quiet place to look at the stars. Let this be your own special time with the Lord. See where it takes you.

3. Is there someone in your life who has followed the call God gave him or her? Ask how God revealed that call and what it took to start living it out. Share with this person your desire to understand God's call in your own life. Pray for God to open your eyes and make His path for you evident. Just wait—you'll begin to see the pieces coming together!

7

THE SIGNATURE

Warning: This chapter is going to get messy. It may poke around at some sore, tender spots in your soul. It may ask questions for which your heart has been begging for answers. It may lead you to a place you never thought you'd go.

We've already talked about the fact that we each have a story. The problem is that with our story comes incredible baggage. Every single one of us carries around a suitcase. Depending on how much junk we are carrying, some may need a wallet and others may need a U-Haul. In this emotional luggage we've packed away parts of our story that have shaped and changed who we are. There is a compartment in our bag that contains the good memories...the things we hold most dear. But the remainder of our bag is taken up by the very things that we wish we could throw away. Our luggage is brimming with shame, rejection, humiliation, past failure, insecurities, ways that we've been wronged, and cutting words that have been said to us—our deepest, darkest scars.

We walk around with these thousand-pound bags strapped to us like a ball and chain. Though it does nothing but weigh us down and break our backs, we have grown attached to our baggage. Its very presence disables us, but we can't imagine being without it. Carrying this bag has become a source of control for us…or at least a way of making sure sure no one else gets their hands on it and peeks at what's inside.

> He is no fool who gives what he cannot keep to gain that which he cannot lose.
>
> —JIM ELLIOT

What are we hiding in our bag that makes us terrified of other people's eyes? What if you opened up your bag and unpacked it—what would you find? Would there be shame? Hurt? Fear? Secrets? Whatever it may be, it must be unpacked. If we are to embark on a journey of discovering our purpose and living a life with meaning, we can't be weighed down by our debilitating luggage.

Daneen's Story

Daneen was four when her father was shot and killed. Though her mother eventually remarried, Daneen never really felt like she grew up with a dad. As a teen, she began trying to fill the void her father left by looking for attention and affirmation from the guys around her. She admits she was always "looking for love in all the wrong places"—places that ultimately lead to trouble.

Though Daneen was raised in church, she said she only went because she was supposed to. Her status as one of her high school's star basketball players landed her in the popular crowd. With this kind of attention, not even the strict rules of her parents could keep her from doing what she wanted. She was 14 when she smoked her first cigarette and began drinking to fit in. The town she lived in was small, and she and her friends partied as "something to do." Little by little, those parties became a lifestyle. She eventually started having sex, and, as she recalls, it was *all* downhill from there.

When Daneen graduated and left home, college became merely an easier way to party. She was away from her parents, all expenses were paid—it was *perfect*. It was here that Daneen opened a treacherous door. Smoking weed became the new addition to her party life. It was all around…everyone did it. Little did she know that weed would be the gateway to a whole lot more pain.

One night Daneen was partying at a club when she was drugged and raped. She learned that she was pregnant—a situation which she quietly "solved" by getting an abortion. Aside from the friend who drove her to the clinic, no one else knew. This was only the beginning of the deep, secret shame that was building up inside of her.

After two and a half years of this lifestyle she was kicked out of college. Her double life couldn't be maintained any longer. She wasn't showing up for class and she had resolved to fail. Academic probation won, and she never returned to school.

Daneen got a job and began dating a guy whom she watched curiously as he put something crushed in his cigarettes. He was a crack addict. Though he warned her not to try it, she didn't listen. She wanted to experience the high for herself.

As Daneen told me this part in her story, regret and pain filled her eyes. "Crack is from the devil," she said. This was the start of a battle for her very life.

Daneen suffered visibly, the effects of crack were too much to hide. Her parents entered her into her first drug rehab, which cleaned her up enough to last four years. But her problem was far from solved. The weight of her baggage was still too much to bear.

As she was trying to get back on her feet again, Daneen found herself being stalked by a man who was obsessed with her. He followed her car one night and ran her off the road into a ditch, where he beat her up badly. Though he went to jail for a short time, when he got out he assured her that he knew where she lived and what she was doing. Daneen was constantly on edge, constantly feeling the need to run. She changed jobs and found a new place to live, but her move unknowingly brought her into the company of people who would bring her even further down. When she started her new job, she had no idea how many drug users worked there. It was enough to break her resolve after four years of staying clean.

As Daneen shared her story and its painful ups and downs, I noticed how every dip in the plot seemed to start with the sentence, "Then I met this guy…" It was so clear that she was continually looking for a "daddy figure." She couldn't be alone. She always had to have a man's affirmation. Sadly, *that's* what was destroying her.

When she met an older man who was the leader of her AA meetings, she thought she had found someone safe. He had been clean for 13 years. But it wasn't long before Daneen learned the real, twisted story: at the same time he was running the rehab meetings, he was underhandedly making a living from *dealing* drugs! This put Daneen right in the thick of it. She began heavily using—even worse than before. And though she never sold drugs herself, her mere presence when he would make deals got her arrested and thrown in federal prison.

Her original sentence was three years for "aiding" in drug deals. But miraculously, her time got pushed back to only one year. She spent the year in a women's federal prison. This was a very sobering time for her, both physically and emotionally. It brought her face-to-face with her choices and the reality of the consequences they were having on her life.

When she was finally released, she was grateful to be given a second chance. But even the treachery of this experience wasn't enough to change her. She still hadn't truly surrendered her life to the Lord.

Meeting another guy and becoming pregnant, she chose to keep her baby. But when the baby's father turned abusive, she didn't know where to turn. "I felt like no one cared about me," she said. "I felt the lowest of low. I didn't care if I lived or not. So I started using crack again, and again."

But when her baby arrived, she knew she *did* have something to live for. This time was different. She wanted a *real* change. This brought her into a Christian rehabilitation program called the Hope Center in Nashville.

She didn't realize until she got there that a large part of the mission center was dedicated to helping the homeless. It was a total culture shock to stay in the same dorm rooms with women off the street. Many smelled funny, looked different, and were mentally ill. "I had to humble myself and realize why I was there," Daneen said. "I was no different. We all needed help—that's why we were there."

This seven-month program took her through a spiritual transformation that affected her like none of the "help" she had received yet. However, this program wasn't her savior. It wasn't until she finally came clean about everything to the people at the Hope Center and her parents that she was finally free. She confessed her abortion and every dark secret she had hidden for all those years. It was ugly, it was messy...but she finally opened up her shameful bag and laid it on the table for them to see. She said, "I *thought* I surrendered to the Lord, but I was still carrying around my shame and secrets in my baggage. I hadn't truly given it all to Him. I would give it and take it back. The last time at rehab, I truly gave it all to God. Until then, the devil had kept me bound by what I held onto."

God confirmed this deliverance to Daneen when she participated in a program called "Seek" at her church. During the month-long experience, participants would wake up extra early every day and find a quiet spot to read, pray, and seek the Lord for a few hours. The experience, she said, was better than any high she had ever had.

On the very last day of the "Seek" month, she heard the Lord softy whisper the words that she had been waiting all her life to hear: *You have been delivered.*

Right then, she knew it was finally over. Her battles, her addictions—she knew it was behind her now. There was no going back; this time was different.

And it was.

Now, Daneen can hardly talk about God and how He has transformed her life without tears filling her eyes. God has restored her. He has redeemed her life from the pit. Daneen is radiant with His beauty and a walking testimony to God's power.

She told me, "My name's still Daneen, but I feel like a completely different person now. I know the Lord and I just cry when I think about Him because I love Him so much."

When I asked her what felt so different, she just said the word *peace*. Her life radiates with joy that she never had before she gave her life to the Lord. Having finally cast off all of the baggage she said, "Nothing can steal my joy. Nothing can bring me down."

Our Wound

> Therefore, since we are surrounded by such a great cloud of witnesses, let us throw off everything that hinders and the sin that so easily entangles. And let us run with perseverance the race marked out for us.
>
> —HEBREWS 12:1

The amazing thing about stories is that we find pieces of ourselves in them. Perhaps as you read Daneen's story, it reminded you of parts of your own. Even if your life and struggles are completely different, you can relate on at least one level...

We all have wounds.

Whether we come from a wonderful, supportive, and loving home or have had a dysfunctional, traumatic upbringing, we all have battle scars. Some of you have wounds the depth of which I can't even begin to imagine. Some of you may have been physically, verbally, or emotionally abused, abandoned by your parents or someone you love, afflicted by a health condition from which you've suffered greatly, or have grown up in a rough neighborhood where you've seen enough violence for a lifetime. Maybe your family had a hard time providing basic necessities. Maybe your family brimmed with wealth, but your mansion was empty of love and never felt like a home. Some of you have gone through the horrific tragedy of losing someone you love. Some of you have never been told that you're loved.

The pain that you've experienced has torn you. It's left you with messy, bleeding wounds. Those raw gashes have left some of you angry and bitter toward God. Some of you, trampled on. Others, hopeless.

I am especially grieved by one thing. Some of you who hold this book in your hands have tried to take your own life. And there are others of you considering it. Oh, dear friends...this breaks my heart! Do you have any idea how precious you are?

God says that you are precious and honored in His sight, and that above all, He *loves* you (Isaiah 43:4). He calls you His chosen one in whom He delights (Isaiah 42:1). He says that nothing could ever separate you from the love that He has for you (Romans 8:38-39).

Let that sink in for a moment. Feel free to put down this book and read those verses for yourself. It's true. His love, His delight, His promises really are for you.

> Praise the Lord, my soul;
>   and forget not all his benefits—
> who forgives all your sins
>   and heals all your diseases,
>   who redeems your life from the pit
>   and crowns you with love and compassion,
> who satisfies your desires with good things
>   so that your youth is renewed like the eagle's...
> For as high as the heavens are above the earth,
>   so great is his love for those who fear him;
>   as far as the east is from the west,
> so far has he removed our transgressions from us.
>   (Psalm 103:2-5,11-12)

Our Most Vulnerable Questions

As much as our hearts may long to believe God's words of affirmation, many of us wrestle with poisoning doubt. What if we are the exception? What if we've missed the part somewhere in the fine print that disqualifies us from His love and grace?

In the midst of our paralyzing fear, we are bombarded with two questions:

Who am I?

What am I worth?

Every person, business, and media outlet in the world vies for the right to answer and decide these questions for us. We are constantly told who we are and are left to infer our worth by the way we are treated. This is why our answers are often messed up.

Who Am I?

You are created. In the Psalms, David reminds us of how we were made. "For you created my inmost being; you knit me together in my mother's womb. I praise you because I am fearfully and wonderfully made; your works are wonderful, I know that full well. My frame was not hidden from you when I was made in the secret place, when I was woven together in the depths of the earth. Your eyes saw my unformed body; all the days ordained for me were written in your book before one of them came to be" (Psalm 139:13-16).

Can you imagine the Lord creating you in Heaven? Can you visualize the way He so carefully took a little of this and just the right amount of that to form you? If you study anatomy, you will understand how intricately, brilliantly, and perfectly your body was made. No accident blew up and poofed you into existence. No, no…*you* are no mistake.

You are known. "You have searched me, LORD, and you know me. You know when I sit and when I rise; you perceive my thoughts from afar. You discern my going out and my lying down; you are familiar with all my ways. Before a word is on my tongue you, LORD, know it completely" (Psalm 139:1-4).

Ever feel like no one understands you? God knows your thoughts before you even think them. He knows you better than you know yourself. God has crafted your personality in such a unique way that He knows every detail of how you are designed to interact with life. He knows your silly quirks, your stubborn habits, your inmost dreams, your deepest fears, and your raw intentions. He knows the things that make you smile and the things you find hysterical. He knows specifically how you desire to be loved, and the ways that the hurtful things in your life have wounded you. He knows the plans that He has for you… the "plans to prosper you and not to harm you, plans to give you hope and a future" (Jeremiah 29:11). He knows you.

You are chosen. "'You are my witnesses,' declares the LORD, 'and my servant whom I have chosen'" (Isaiah 43:10). "In Him we were also chosen, having been predestined according to the plan of him who works out everything in conformity with the purpose of his will" (Ephesians

1:11). "You are a chosen people, a royal priesthood, a holy nation, God's special possession, that you may declare the praises of him who called you out of darkness into his wonderful light" (1 Peter 2:9).

We are chosen to be His servant, and in that, we have been given the greatest role of a lifetime. Through Him, we have the power and opportunity to free captives, shake nations, and move mountains (Matthew 17:20). Nothing is impossible with Him by our side. God doesn't need us, He chose us.

You are identified. "The Spirit testifies with our spirit that we are God's children. Now if we are children, then we are heirs—heirs of God and co-heirs with Christ" (Romans 8:16-17).

Your social security number only goes so far. Any nickname, title, or idea that someone has of you doesn't scratch the surface of defining you. When it comes to your true identity—the core of who you really are—you are God's child. The son, the daughter of the King. You are the ultimate royalty, of utmost worth. Your given name is overshadowed by your true title…Prince, Princess. You are His!

You are purposed. "For we are the product of His hand, heaven's poetry etched on lives, created in Jesus, the Liberator, to accomplish the good works God arranged long ago" (Ephesians 2:10 The Voice).

We are placed on this earth for a reason that God mapped out long before we existed. We are history waiting to happen. You and I have been strategically placed in this point in time. The way that God has created us is specifically linked to the purpose for which we are here. He has equipped each of us in a unique way to live out the calling, the work that He prepared for us long ago. Our strengths, and even our weaknesses, are handcrafted to fit our purpose.

What Am I Worth?

There was a time several years ago when every day, several times a day, I begged God to show me what I was worth. For whatever reason, I felt my worth being attacked more than I ever had in my life. Everything around me fought to diminish who I felt I was and what I was capable of. This feeling got so bad that on some days I could hardly get out of bed…or even off the floor. "If I am worth anything, show me what I'm worth," I cried to the Lord.

Where was this feeling of total diminished value coming from? Unlike the stories of so many others, I had loving parents, supportive friends, a foundation in God…where was I getting this message?

I believe somewhere deep inside each one of us, Satan has planted the idea that we are worthless, unlovable, and irredeemable. These ideas are packaged in an individual way, intertwining with whatever struggle or weakness is specific to us. During the time that I felt attacked by these feelings of worthlessness, I was at a place where God was beginning to open some big doors for me in ministry. I was getting ready to go on the road to talk with others about the value they had in Christ, yet ironically, that was the very area in which I was being attacked.

Each night as I shared the message on stage, I felt the encouragement that God had put on my heart to share with others come flooding back to me. I believed those words wholeheartedly for everyone else, but He was reminding me that they were real for me too.

What is at the heart of your question—"What am I worth?"

Have you found your answer from the person who's abused you? Have you found your answer from the way you despise yourself? Have you found your answer in the silence of those you asked to affirm you?

We could build a tower a mile high with all of the answers to this question that we've collected along the way, but there is only one answer, one true authority over our deepest question.

What does *God* say you are worth?

He says that you are worth the death of His one and only Son. He says that you are worth the shame of rejection, the humility of belittling Himself among His creation, and the unimaginable, excruciating pain of being whipped to near death and then ruthlessly nailed to a cross. *He says that you are worth everything He had.*

Jesus didn't only die for your salvation, that you might have eternal life through Him. He died for your shame. He died for your guilt, your pain. His life for our life. He feels that was a fair trade.

I have swept away your offenses like a cloud, your sins like the morning mist. Return to me, for I have redeemed you (Isaiah 44:22).

Repent, Return, Restore

No matter how filthy, bruised, or beaten down you may be, God wants to rebuild you. He wants to take every little shattered piece in your life and not only put you back together but make you whole—as if you had never been broken. He wants to do a new thing in you—give you a new life, a healed heart, a fresh start.

The Lord assures you in Jeremiah 31:3-4, "I have loved you with an everlasting love; Therefore I have drawn you with lovingkindness. Again I will build you and you will be rebuilt" (NASB).

If you have reached the end of your rope, it is time to surrender. If you are too weak to get off the ground, you are at the perfect place to meet God. It is only on our knees that we can submit our brokenness and truly see His face.

If you've been running, resisting, or rebelling, God's heart cries for you to repent. You will never be satisfied or made whole if you reject the very thing that your heart and life was created for: Him.

"This is how much God loved the world: He gave his Son, his one and only Son. And this is why: so that no one need be destroyed; by believing in him, anyone can have a whole and lasting life. God didn't go to all the trouble of sending his Son merely to point an accusing finger, telling the world how bad it was. He came to help, to put the world right again. Anyone who trusts in him is acquitted; anyone who refuses to trust him has long since been under the death sentence without knowing it. And why? Because of that person's failure to believe in the one-of-a-kind Son of God when introduced to him" (John 3:16-18 MSG).

God is not extending a hand of condemnation. He is extending life! *Receive it.*

> Do not fear, for I have redeemed you; I have summoned you by name; you are mine.
>
> —ISAIAH 43:1

The Signature

In the days before presidents and parliaments, a king would use a special seal to represent his signature. This seal was unmistakably his, and he would use it to mark the documents that he approved or claimed as his own. No one would dare touch or argue with anything marked by the king's seal. Its worth was unmatched, and its importance unprecedented. Nothing could come against the seal.

You and I have the seal of the one true King on us.

"Because you have believed in the One who is truth, your lives are marked with His seal" Ephesians 1:13 (The Voice). If we call Him Lord and surrender our lives, He places His Spirit in us—His very own seal.

The signature of the King is inscribed on you. Lift up your head; it is crowned with royalty.

ACTION CHALLENGE

1. Have you handed all of your baggage over to Him? Is there pain you are still holding onto? Surrender completely before Him. It is only then that you can truly be restored.

2. Ask the Lord to make Himself and His love real to you in a way you have never experienced before. Let the revelation of His incredible love lead you into His arms.

3. Close this book and reflect on what you just read. Grab your Bible and read Isaiah 43:1-19 and Psalm 103.

8

TWO FEET DON'T
MAKE A HAND

I t was almost spring, and Sarah's school was getting ready for its annual talent show. She was a junior and each year that they had the event, she found herself fascinated by it and secretly wishing for a talent that would qualify her to enter. Her school was large and the amount and variety of talent within it was immense. Each year the faculty picked only the best of the best to perform, so the stakes were high.

The closest Sarah ever came to the talent show was living vicariously through her friend Rachelle, who was put in charge of organizing the event that year and coordinating the details. Because of this, Sarah came to know the ins and outs of how things were set up, planned, and decided upon, leading up to the main event. There was something about this process that got her all fired up—something that she couldn't explain, but she knew she loved.

One evening Sarah got a call from Rachelle.

"Sarah…I just got terrible news. My grandfather passed away tonight and I have to fly to Texas the week of the talent show for his memorial service. I can't miss this. Could you take my place and handle the event?"

Sarah choked slightly on her gasped air. Silence hit the airwaves for a moment until it was broken by her shaky voice. "…You want me to organize the talent show?"

"Yes, of course! There's really no other student who knows as much about the way this program works that I could trust handing it off to. I think you're the perfect person," Rachelle assured her confidently.

Sarah bit her lip, knowing her friend was right. No other student had sat in on the planning year after year like she had. They were only two weeks away from the event, and if she didn't step up, who would? Before she let her thoughts talk her out of it, she agreed and told Rachelle that she would do her best to complete the job.

Over the next two weeks, Sarah stepped into a role that she had never been given before. Suddenly she was in charge of meetings, decisions, and even people! The authority that she had been given made her nervous sometimes, but at the same time, she liked it. As the demands of planning the event hustled and bustled each day, she found that she thrived on coordinating everything and taking care of the details. Her newly found organizational and managerial skills made the job easier. She was more of a natural than she ever thought she could be. Not only did she find that she was good at this kind of event planning, but that she thoroughly enjoyed it!

When it finally came to the night of the event, the whole show played out beautifully. The contestants were superb (as usual), but there was a new talent in the group that really set this event apart from all of the others: Sarah. The transitions were seamless, the light and sound operators hit their cues, and the presenters had performed perfectly. The whole show had gone off without a hitch! The faculty knew who was behind this and honored Sarah for her hard work, unexpected skill, and dedication.

Sarah couldn't believe it. The event that she had admired from the sidelines for years she had now *planned!* She always thought that the talent show was merely for the people who had…well, talent. She couldn't sing, dance, juggle, write poetry, or do really anything worthy of securing her a spot to perform on stage. What she learned is that not all talents are expressed the same way. When she finally realized that it wasn't performing that she had a passion for, but planning, she felt like she had been given the key to her soul.

Sarah had found her niche. After all her middle school and high school years of searching, she finally found the place where she belonged.

The Gift in All of Us

Have you ever wondered if you have a talent? Have you worried that you're not good at anything? As tempting as it might seem to look at your prodigy brother and think that you got gypped in the family talent genes, you were given a brilliant, unique set of gifts that are specific to you. Though not all gifts are initially as noticeable as others, every single one of us has them…and not one person has been left out. "Into every heart, God wisely assembled a set of gifts and talents uniquely designed to fulfill one specific destiny. Implicit in this action is a charge to you: Know who you are and use what He has given you to speak to the world."*

Our talents are not just about "being good at something," but are instilled in us for a much bigger, better reason. Our gifts pave our life's road and are the tools with which we live out our purpose. They aren't just for decoration…they are to be used, expanded, and generously given.

In the Bible, God refers to each of our gifts as parts of a larger movement. We, as God's church, make up what the apostle Paul calls the body of Christ: "We are like the various parts of a human body. Each part gets its meaning from the body as a whole, not the other way around. The body we're talking about is Christ's body of chosen people. Each of us finds our meaning and function as a part of his body. But as a chopped-off finger or cut-off toe we wouldn't amount to much, would we? So since we find ourselves fashioned into all these excellently formed and marvelously functioning parts in Christ's body, let's just go ahead and be what we were made to be, without enviously or

---

* Lila Empson and Bryan Norman, eds., *The New Rebellion Handbook* (Brentwood, TN: Thomas Nelson Inc., 2006), 71.

pridefully comparing ourselves with each other, or trying to be something we aren't" (Romans 12:4-6 MSG).

We are part of something bigger than ourselves. Yet at the same time, each of our roles are irreplaceable. Just as our bodies can't function properly without our leg, nose, or eye, so the body of Christ can't function properly without you. First Corinthians 12:18-20,27 says, "But in fact God has arranged the parts of the body, every one of them, just as he wanted them to be. If they were all one part, where would the body be? As it is, there are many parts, but one body…Now you are the body of Christ, and each one of you is a part of it."

If each one of us is a part in this body of Christ, then what God wants to give through each one of us is essential! We individually bring something different to the whole—something that the rest of the body struggles to function without. What beautiful proof that each one of us is charged with a special purpose!

One of the things that makes every gift so special is that each one is an attribute of God Himself. The Creator of the Universe has entrusted us with pieces of Himself to live out in this world. As The Message translation of the Bible puts it, "Each person is given something to do that shows who God is: Everyone gets in on it, everyone benefits. All kinds of things are handed out by the Spirit, and to all kinds of people! The variety is wonderful" (1 Corinthians 12:7).

How does it make you feel to know that who you are is a piece of the image of God Himself?

The Reason Why

We are on a journey to find our purpose. That's what this is all about. It's a deep digging process to take a look at our story, unpack our baggage, reclaim our value, and discover our gifts. We do this so that we may find the fire in our souls. Too many of us have been walking blind, not sure where we fit or why we're here…and it's time for that to change. If we are placed on this earth for a reason, it's time to find out why, and what we're going to do about it.

A 15-year-old girl once told me her story. She was anorexic, a cutter, and suicidal. She was sent to a rehabilitation center, and it was there that she began to heal. Her healing, however, didn't come just from the right drugs or therapy, but from encouraging the other patients. After reaching out to one girl in particular, she found purpose and passion in the ability to help other people through their pain. She said when she got home, "I don't want to hurt myself anymore because I want to make a difference."

What amazing hope our purpose gives. Purpose can save our very lives!

This is why we seek to find and live out our gifts—not only because people will be changed, but because as we live them out, we fulfill God's plan to heal our hearts and make us into the whole man or woman that He desires us to be.

How Do I Find My Gift?

Just as there is an innumerable variety of gifts, there are many different ways that we can discover our gifts. Some people's gifts are obvious from the time they come out of the womb. Others seem to go through a little bit of life before they discover what they're drawn to and what they're good at. There are even those who find their gifts and passion through pain—their trial brings about a part of them, some strength or convcition, which they hadn't known existed.

> "Each of you should use whatever gift you have received to serve others, as faithful stewards of God's grace in its various forms."
> —1 PETER 4:10

As we seek to understand our purpose, our passion goes hand in hand. We will dive into our passion in a later chapter, but for now let's tackle our gifts. Brainstorm with me a little!

What do you love to do more than anything?

When do you feel most in your element?

What inspires you?

If you had 3 hours to do any activity in the world, what would you do? (Note: your answer cannot be "sleeping," "Internet-surfing," or "doing nothing.")

Have you ever received repeated compliments on your ability to do one specific thing? If so, what?

Is there anything that you do that comes surprisingly easily or naturally to you that you've noticed isn't as easy for some others?

These are just general brainstorming questions to get you thinking. Don't panic if you don't know the answers. This is a process, and it's not always instant. I will say, however, that deep down each one of us does have these answers. We just may not recognize them yet within ourselves.

Though we have to be careful about listening to people's opinions of us, we can learn a lot from a person we deeply trust, who knows us and has our best interest in mind. If there is a person like this in your life, perhaps you can ask them what special gifts and abilities they see in you. Pray about what they share and see if that is something you feel lines up with what God is telling you and the inkling you have in your soul. Once you have an idea of what these gifts may be, test them out! See how others respond when you use them and how it makes you feel in the process. Does this gift benefit others? Does it bring joy to you? When you use it, are you honoring the Lord?

My friend Wes shared with me some of his journey toward finding his gifts. He said, "God told my mom when she was pregnant with me that I was going to be musical and be a writer. Even as a young child, I would plunk at pianos and try to play instruments. The writing part came after my family moved from Holland to the United States. I didn't know anybody there, so I picked up the guitar and spent the summer teaching myself to play. As I taught myself guitar, lyrics began to flow along with the music I was creating. I was 13 the first time I ever played something that I wrote in public, and it was for a memorial service for a miscarried child. While the circumstance was unexpected and could have been uncomfortable, it was amazing in that it wasn't about me. My role was genuinely about the people there being comforted. That was the moment I realized I wanted to write music to speak for people who don't have words."

I want to share another story of a dear older friend, Mary. She didn't discover her gifts as instantly and obviously as Wes did. Growing up, her parents never encouraged her to pursue anything or praised any of her talents or abilities. For her, the road to knowing her gifts has been slow, at times frustrating, and often lonely. Mary came to know the Lord later in her life, and reflects that though she didn't understand or consider that the Lord had placed gifts within her to use, she unknowingly used many of them throughout her life. The qualities that she now recognizes as gifts God has given her are creativity, incredible cooking abilities, an eye for style and design, compassion, hospitality, and a counseling voice and listening ear. Though she unknowingly used those gifts along the way throughout her life, the thing that she regrets most is that the whole time she had no idea she was truly gifted. For all those years, she never received the fulfillment of knowing that God was using her, that she had a purpose and what she offered was of great worth. Had she known, not only would she have developed those gifts a lot earlier with more intention, but she would have spared herself the pain of feeling unfulfilled along the way.

Mary's story reveals an understated and vital part of finding our gifts: the impact it has on us personally. Ultimately, *knowing* that God has given us gifts is the first step in discovering them. And if we have a relationship with the Lord, *asking* Him to reveal to us what they are is the second. God desires for us to know the valuable tools that He has placed in us so we might use them for His glory and be personally fulfilled by His work in and through us.

The Three Essential Parts

As you look inside yourself for these gifts, you're trying to answer three questions: *What* are my gifts? *Why* were they given to me? *How* do I use them? These questions can be answered by taking a closer look at your talents, spiritual gifts, and personality. Let's take a look.

Our talents. These are the ones we think of most when we're faced with the question, "What are you good at?" But let's be sure that our idea isn't misguided—there are many more kinds of talent than can be displayed on *American Idol* or a stage. Here are some ideas to get you started, but remember—this is barely scratching the surface! Circle any of the bold words that you feel apply to you—then, any applicable descriptions within them. As another way of thinking of it, which are the ones you enjoy the most?

- **Organizing**—this could mean groups of people, events, or just being neat and tidy

- **Technical work**—skill with computers, electronics, etc.

- **Designing**—this could be fashion, graphic design, architecture, products, etc.

- **Creating**—this could be art, film, writing, photography, music, or cooking

- **Performing**—music, dance, acting, speaking, anything that involves getting up in front of others

- **Action**—sports, physical labor, building, working out, etc.

- **Traveling**—the love of going different places and experiencing new things

- **Learning**—the love of knowledge, studying, and exploring

- **Serving**—this can include hospitality, secretary work, behind-the-scenes work

- **Numbers**—problem solving, being math-minded, analytical

- **Communicating**—relational, loving conversation, and connecting with people

- **Marketing**—promoting, selling people on something, being convincing

- **Investigating**—exploring, digging deeper into details and solving/proving things

- **Counseling**—listening, offering advice, helping

- **Humor**—the ability to make people laugh

- **Enterprising**—business minded, always on the rise, full of ideas

- **Fixing**—skilled at working with hands, putting things together, or fixing

- **Providing**—being generously aware of others' needs and giving to them whenever able

- **Nurturing**—taking care of others, helping others grow

- **Sharing**—this could be teaching, volunteering, spending time giving to others

- **Protecting**—watching out for others using physical or mental strength to defend the helpless or vulnerable

Take a look at the words you circled. Were you already aware of those interests/abilities in yourself? Were there some things on the list that you were surprised were actually considered gifts? When it comes to our purpose and how we are to specifically live it out, our talents are our *what*.

Our spiritual gifts. These are the *why* behind everything that we do. This is what we build our life's mission around. Our spiritual gifts relate to our passion, and are the most fulfilling part of our gifts. This is where God has placed little pieces of Himself in us. The Bible talks about many different kinds of spiritual gifts, but the main ones mentioned are:

- **Administration** (1 Corinthians 12:28)
- **Discernment** (1 Corinthians 12:10)
- **Evangelism** (Ephesians 4:11-13)
- **Exhortation/Encouragement** (Romans 12:8)
- **Faith** (1 Corinthians 12:9)
- **Giving** (Romans 12:8)
- **Helping/Hospitality** (1 Corinthians 12:28, Romans 12:13)
- **Knowledge** (1 Corinthians 12:8)
- **Leadership** (Romans 12:6)
- **Mercy** (Romans 12:8)
- **Pastoring/Shepherding** (Ephesians 4:11-13)
- **Prophecy** (1 Corinthians 12:10,28)
- **Serving** (Romans 12:7)
- **Healing/Miracles/Tongues** (1 Corinthians 12:9-10,28)
- **Teaching** (1 Corinthians 12:28)
- **Wisdom** (1 Corinthians 12:8)

Each of us has a unique grouping of the spiritual gifts that we are strongest in. Similarly, we each have a grouping that we are weakest in! But all of these gifts are good. No one has received the short end of the stick or a less desirable gift. Every single one of these spiritual gifts is honorable and essential to the proper functioning of the body of Christ.

If you are curious as to which of the spiritual gifts you have, I encourage you to take a spiritual gifts test either through your church or online. There are some great free tests online, and if you go to www.paigeomartian.com and click on the Chapter 8 section, you will find a few that I recommend.

Keep in mind, however, these free online tests may not be perfectly accurate. Some of the online tests tend to be a bit shorter and less in-depth, but can at least be a good start if you are curious and have never taken one. Most churches have a resource for their congregation of more in-depth spiritual gift tests, so I would advise you to check with your church to see if they have one that you can take for a more accurate assessment.

I was in a Bible study that did a spiritual gifts test a few years ago and I found it incredibly helpful and eye-opening to go through the multiple-choice questions and read my assessment. I learned that my top four spiritual gifts are exhortation (encouragement), pastoring/shepherding, mercy, and wisdom. While initially I might not have expected to see those gifts on my list, I found that once I took a deeper look at the meanings of each one, they really did represent my heart and the way that I naturally tend to go about things.

I want to be careful to add that spiritual gifts are something for which we need to seek the Lord first and foremost and an outside source in addition to the test we take. It is important that others bear witness to evidence of these gifts in our life. Once you are able to identify them, it is so much easier to know your place in a group, not to mention in *life*, and offer the gifts God has given you to the world.

Our personality. The third essential element is one that is most definitely an overlooked part of our gifting. While our personality at times may seem like a more mood-driven part of us, it actually holds very intentional and distinct characteristics that are just as important as the rest of our gifts.

If you've ever been known as shy, outgoing, or even strong-willed, know that these characteristics are a part of your special personality makeup. While there are many ways to dive into the depths of decoding our personality, one of the most long-standing and respected authorities in this area is called the Myers-Briggs Type Indicator (MBTI). This is the most widely used personality test in the world. The basis of their personality assessment is centered on these four preferences. In each of these categories, circle one of the two options that seems to best describe you.*

Where do you direct your focus?

Extroversion (E): If you prefer to direct your focus on dealing with people, things, situations, or "the outer world," then your preference is for Extroversion.

Introversion (I): If you prefer to direct your focus on dealing with ideas, information, explanations or beliefs, or "the inner world," then your preference is for Introversion.

How do you process information?

Sensing (S): If you prefer to deal with facts, what you know, having clarity, or describing what you see, then your preference is for Sensing.

Intuition (N): If you prefer to deal with ideas, looking into the unknown, developing new possibilities, or anticipating what isn't obvious, then your preference is for Intuition.

How do you make decisions?

Thinking (T): If you prefer to make decisions on the basis of objective logic, using an analytical and detached approach, then your preference is for Thinking.

Feeling (F): If you prefer to make decisions using values and/or personal beliefs, on the basis of what you believe is important or what you or others care about, then your preference is for Feeling.

---

* The Myers & Briggs Foundation, "MBTI® Basics," accessed October 27, 2011, http://www.myersbriggs.org/my-mbti-personality-type/mbti-basics/.

How do you organize your life?

Judging (J): If you prefer your life to be planned, stable, and organized then your preference is for Judging.

Perceiving (P): If you prefer to go with the flow, maintain flexibility, and respond to situations as they arise, then your preference is for Perceiving.

Once you have chosen your four preferences, write down the corresponding letters in a row. For example, mine looks like ENFJ. There are 16 different combinations of letters, and each combination represents a separate personality type. For the description of your personality preference, go to my website and click on the Chapter 8 tab. It will guide you to where you can find the meaning behind your grouping of letters.

> Whatever the circumstance of your life, the understanding of your personality can make your perceptions clearer, your judgments sounder, and your life closer to your heart's desire.
>
> —*ISABEL BRIGGS MYERS*

Our personalities are not only different, they're intentional. God made us this way, with these preferences and ways of going about life to specifically fit the calling He has for us. This is the *how* in living out our purpose—our personality sets the tone for how the rest of our gifts come across!

God so wisely chooses these gifts and personality combinations for us because of the important way in which they work together. Does this make you feel like you're not an accident just thrown together after all? Does it speak to how complex and planned you are that you have to take the time to actually dissect and decode your own self? There's something very revealing about that!

What Now?

Perhaps this chapter has left your head spinning with all of the information, links, tests, and letters that have just been dumped out. Perhaps it leaves you with a lingering question...what do I do now?

Have you ever heard the story of Jesus feeding the 5,000? Jesus was ready to go and rest in a solitary place when people spotted Him and formed a crowd around Him. Jesus had compassion on the people, so He began to teach and share with them. As it became later in the day, the disciples asked Jesus to send the people back to the countryside or their villages to get something to eat. Perhaps they were worried that chaos could ensue with a hungry mob so late in the evening!

To the disciples' surprise (and I imagine, dismay), Jesus answered them, "They do not need to go away. *You* give them something to eat" (Matthew 14:16, emphasis added).

They quickly protested, "That would take more than half a year's wages! Are we to go and spend that much on bread and give it to them to eat?"

"How many loaves do you have?" Jesus replied. "Go and see" (Mark 6:37-38).

Andrew, one of His disciples, spoke up, saying, "Here is a boy with five small barley loaves and two small fish, but how far will they go among so many?"

Jesus had the crowd of 5,000 sit down as He took the loaves, gave thanks, and distributed them to those who were seated. When they had all had enough to eat, He had the disciples gather the pieces that were left over. There were 12 basketfuls (John 6:8-13).

> Your talent is God's gift to you. What you do with it is your gift back to God.
>
> —LEO BUSCAGLIA

Picture this: There are people in great need. God has heard their cries and desires to shower them with help and compassion. He calls upon you, His servant, to go with Him and on His behalf to be the tangible, physical help and comfort that these people need. You, seeing the situation as utterly impossible according to the means that you have, tell the Lord that you have no way of helping—you're simply not equipped. He asks you in response,

"Well, what *do* you have?" You shyly hold out your hand with the few gifts that you've been given. He looks at your hands and smiles. "Perfect," He says. "This will be *more* than enough."

What if so many of the ways that God desires to serve the world lay within the clenched fingers of our hands? What if we realized that what we have on our own isn't enough, yet what we do have when we open our hands and give it to Him will leave the world overflowing?

May this discovery of the gifts you hold in your hand leave you willing to open them.

You have *so* much to give.

ACTION CHALLENGE

1. Be sure you have completed all of the exercises in this chapter in order to get the most out of it. Go to www.paigeomartian.com and take the suggested spiritual gifts and personality tests. Find out how God has specifically shaped *you*.

2. Ask the Lord to reveal the gifts He's given you in various ways. Let this be a fun and exciting process of uncovering who He has made you to be!

9

COME ALIVE

When I was a little girl, I used to wander around the creek in our yard, searching for adventures and humming a melody of my own creation as a soundtrack. An exciting world awaited, and I was dying to discover, understand, and unveil it. Everything was a dramatic, unsolved mystery to me. The grass, a tree, rocks, a pile of dirt…everything had a story. Eager to play a role of my own, I stepped into the story as if it had invited me in.

As I played out my magical escapades, I secretly hoped some prince would heroically discover me and join me in my adventure. My idea of romance was exhilarating, mysterious, epic…and I played the role of the beauty. Regardless of the prince's role in my story, however, I was on a journey. A mission. There was something to be done that was far beyond both of us.

The sky was my endless inspiration. Even after hours outside, when my imagination grew tired and I had explored all of the trees and rocks and creeks and crevices and creatures possible, one look at the sky reminded me that there was so much more to dream. I had only just begun. In my exploits, there was always someone to save, something broken to restore, or something lost that needed to be returned. The adventure was never over.

Many years later, I sat in a little tree house and reflected on those childhood adventures. I had climbed up into the little hideout for some time to myself. I went there to sort out some of the big, adult things I was facing, but instead I found myself, unexpectedly, reminiscing about my childhood. As I looked at the playground and reflected on my escapades, I found that deep down, my heart still wanted to see life as I did then. Each day was a mission that really did involve something broken or lost (only now, it was people rather than rocks), and I desired to play a dangerously exciting part in it. The only difference in my story was that now, I wasn't as good at dreaming. My mind had limits on it that it never used to have. Though in my heart I was still the curious, adventurous, and hopeful little girl, somewhere along the way I had become jaded with harsh and cold messages that had shut down the fire I once held inside.

Somewhere in my story I had been told that adventures and dreams won't get you anywhere—that only what is practical, apparent, or "industry standard" is accepted. I'd been told that what is lost and broken isn't worth saving, that it's better off where it was left. I'd been told that I wasn't worth discovering, that who I am could never be captivating. But see, I think I'd merely encountered the villain in the story. Had I forgotten who's on the winning side?

Taking Back Our Dreams

Have you ever had a dream? When you were a kid, did you have an unlimited imagination that convinced you that you could build your own wings and fly? Sure, sometimes that may have gotten you into a little bit of trouble. But overall, it was a pretty good thing!

I believe somewhere in our early teen years, right about the time when the idea of being "cool" slips in, we lose the sense of wonder and unlimited thinking that we were born with. The first time our dreams are trampled, our heart is crushed, or a bitter reality is revealed, something inside of us dies. Reasoning that it's just part of growing up, we trade in our larger-than-life dreams for a random major in college and a job we figure is "good enough."

When considering what we should do with our lives, most of us think of the practical, realistic options of how to make a living. Rarely are we encouraged to pursue our biggest dreams or discover our innermost passions! Instead, we get placed on something I like to call the "conveyor belt of life." This belt only has one route, and it seems to set the rule for how things are supposed to go. According to this rule, there is no other way.

At some point in time we are all on a conveyor belt. Whether it's our family's, society's, or one built of our circumstances, we all get pulled onto a moving track of expectations and pre-set rules. Some people think as long as it's moving and other people are on it, it's the safest route to go. What they don't realize is that riding on the conveyor belt lulls you into a lethargic state of motivationless, lifeless existence.

Stepping off the Moving Track

When we don't have a goal or vision to follow, we are instantly swept onto the moving track of the conveyor belt. If you've ever felt like you're coasting through life with no direction, you know the feeling. Suddenly you end up someplace you don't want to be and can't figure out how you got there or what you're supposed to be doing there. All you know is that the conveyor belt keeps moving.

When we don't surrender our life to the Lord, we unknowingly surrender it to other things. No longer are we seeking what the Lord desires for us, let alone hearing what He's trying to say.

In Matthew 7:13-14 Jesus teaches us to "enter through the narrow gate. For wide is the gate and broad is the road that leads to destruction, and many enter through it. But small is the gate and narrow the road that leads to life, and only a few find it."

If you've ever been in line at a massive concert trying to make your way through the main doors, it's not hard to know where to go! Just follow the crowd. But if you even so much as turn the wrong direction you'll be trampled and dragged through the door like gum on someone's shoe—there's no stopping; the line is moving!

If you were called to the VIP entrance, you'd definitely have to know where you were going in order to find the special entrance that only a handful of people were entering. If you weren't paying careful attention, it would sure be easy to miss!

Unlike the VIP entrance, you don't even need to have your eyes open to get through the main concert door. The swiftly moving crowd will practically carry you in themselves. This is what happens in life. We shut our eyes to where we're going and just hope some current will take us to a place we'll like. Many have lost the spark that once set our soul ablaze and don't even dream of stepping onto a path that is intentionally our own. Our life is mediocre at best, and we know it. We think it must be nice for those who actually have adventure, excitement, and fulfillment in their lives, because we feel certain that blasé is what we're destined to be.

No More Lukewarm

Many of us have traded in the fire within us for a lukewarm heart. Those who are lukewarm have chosen, knowingly or unknowingly, to settle for less—not only in the realm of how they live their life, but in their relationship with God.

One of the best books I've read addressing a lukewarm attitude toward life and God is called *Crazy Love*, by Francis Chan. In his chapter "Profile of the Lukewarm," he describes characteristics of those who have succumbed to this kind of a mindset and lifestyle. Check out what he has to say:

> Lukewarm People are continually concerned with playing it safe; they are slaves to the god of control. This focus on safe living keeps them from sacrificing and risking for God...Lukewarm People do not live by faith; their lives are structured so that they never have to. The truth is, their lives wouldn't look much different if they suddenly stopped believing in God.*

---

* Francis Chan, *Crazy Love: Overwhelmed by a Relentless God* (Colorado Springs: David C. Cook, 2008), 75-76.

Yikes! This is convicting. And this is exactly what living life on the conveyor belt does to us. While we think and feel safe because we are on the same track as a ton of other people, we have no idea it is leading us to destruction. Our eyes are closed! Worst of all, we have removed our need for God. We are calling our own shots, and prefer to ride the track we're on to whatever destination may come.

Brakes. Halt. Stop.

Do you see what has happened? Those who are drifting through life lukewarm are not even living!

The Lord says in Revelation 3:1-2, "I know your deeds; you have a reputation of being alive, but you are dead. Wake up!" and continues in verses 15-16, "I know your deeds, that you are neither cold nor hot. I wish you were either one or the other! So, because you are lukewarm—neither hot nor cold—I am about to spit you out of my mouth."

Now *that's* what I call a strong statement. The Lord would rather have us be cold toward Him, moving in completely the opposite direction, than to be half-heartedly committed to Him and lukewarm with our lives. He goes as far as to say that if we are lukewarm He will spit us out of His mouth! He simply can't tolerate it. God has created us to brim with life and be on fire for Him. He can't bear to see the indifference in our hearts!

God made you and me to spice up the world. We are to be salt and light and evidence of His awesome power here on earth. The last thing that Christians should be, though we have developed a sad reputation for this, is boring, apathetic, uncreative, dull, unmotivated, and lifeless. When looking for the fruit of Christ in our life, I reason that those kinds of qualities leave no evidence of Him at all!

"Salt is good, but if it loses its saltiness, how can it be made salty again? It is fit neither for the soil nor for the manure pile; it is thrown out" (Luke 14:34-35). Not only do lukewarm Christians smear Christ's reputation with their lack of spiritual passion, they sit in a puddle of mediocrity that won't begin to scratch the surface of what their life could have been. Jesus never demonstrated a life that was safe, normal, or even practical. He lived a life that was radical.

Jesus, Our Radical Example

Jesus turned the world upside down on the first day He came into it. He was on a mission—there was no messing around. Starting at age 12, He began engaging in conversations with important religious leaders and leaving them completely baffled by His wisdom and understanding of Scripture. Everything that Jesus did was out of the ordinary, unexpected. He devoted Himself to people—healing them, teaching them, loving them, and meeting them right where they were. He broke the man-made rules that went against God's rules, called people out on their hypocrisy, befriended the outcasts, and offered salvation to the prostitutes. He told people backward things—the weak are strong, the last shall be first, love your enemies, your trials are blessings, and your hope is unseen. Talk about unusual.

> If life is a river, then pursuing Christ requires swimming upstream. When we stop swimming, or actively following Him, we automatically begin to be swept downstream.
>
> —*FRANCIS CHAN*

As we read the Gospels, we see that everything about Jesus was radical. Everything about Him was completely different from what anyone had ever seen. Yes, He is the Son of God—of course He is different! But we are called to follow in His steps. To imitate Him, represent Him, and be ambassadors for Him on this earth. The disciples He gathered during His ministry are examples of how we are supposed to lay down our lives and radically follow Him. Consider what legends these disciples have become—how their sold-out lives changed the course of history and have laid the foundation for the Church. These average men left their ordinary lives behind, exchanging them for an extraordinary calling that would utterly change the world. If God could use 12 ordinary men, how much more could He do with 50, 100, 1,000 of us if we choose to lay down our lives to radically serve Him?

The World at Our Fingertips

The first time I read the quote below, I was astounded. It's not saying we should disregard what the world needs. It's saying we shouldn't build our lives around what we think everyone else wants us to be. Dare to find that dream inside of you and be passionate about it! Come alive to the fire God has placed inside your soul!

I recently had the privilege of visiting and working in the Dominican Republic with Compassion International. This was my first ministry trip out of the country, and I witnessed poverty and need like I never had before. All of the pictures and stories I'd always heard of hungry children and people living in barely fastened-together shacks became real. I *met* those children. I *went into* those shacks. As I rode along in the bus that took my team into different villages, I couldn't help but watch the people we drove by on the dirt and garbage-filled streets. Many of them, standing on the side of the road or in front of their near-in-ruins homes, looked as though they had no idea how to hope. Dreaming was a luxury they couldn't even afford.

> Don't ask yourself what the world needs. Ask yourself what makes you come alive, and go and do that, because what the world needs is people who have come alive.
>
> —GIL BAILIE

If you're like me, you grew up with the idea that you could be whatever you wanted to be. You could change your mind every day because you had so many options. In a second you could choose to be a doctor, a lawyer, a singer, a chef, a banker, a physical therapist, an astronaut, a filmmaker—whatever you wanted!

The precious people I met in the Dominican—and millions of others around the world—need a miracle just to be given the chance to dream like we can.

The irony is that you and I have every option of education, entrepreneurial opportunities, and career paths right in front of us, yet such a tragic number could seemingly care less. We feel our endless choices are more a burden than a blessing, and we'd rather not be bothered with figuring it all out.

This is crazy. You and I have the world at our fingertips. Do we even realize it?

One of my favorite parts of traveling to the Dominican was meeting the students who had been sponsored through Compassion International's Leadership Development Program to go to college. These students told us how hard they worked in order to make the cut for eligibility. For them, this was the only way to get out of poverty.

> One of life's greatest tragedies is a person with a 10-by-12 capacity and a 2-by-4 soul.
>
> —DR. KENNETH HILDEBRAND

I was astounded by the gratitude and seriousness with which they approached their career and life calling. After the opportunities they'd been given, they knew they had a responsibility to help their communities in return. Many of them were the first in their families to have the chance to pursue an education and career.

Not only do you and I have no reason not to live the dreams that God has called us to, but coming from our unlimited opportunities, we have no *excuse* not to. There is no dream too big, no idea too complex, no problem too great when the Lord is standing by our side, whispering in our ear that He promises to do the impossible. Satan would love nothing more than to snuff out the fire in your soul and tell you all the reasons why you will never accomplish anything!

Let me tell you a secret...

He's just scared.

"For the Spirit God gave us does not make us timid, but gives us power, love and self-discipline" (2 Timothy 1:7). Within each of us who know Christ is a power through Him that we cannot even fathom. For the God who hung the stars, tossed down the oceans, and created the universe, accomplishing your wildest dreams is but a mere wave of the hand. It is not a matter of whether or not He will carry out this work in you. It is a matter of whether you will choose to step up and accept the role He has already given you. Will you come alive to the radical, breathtaking life that He offers?

There Is No Plan B

I was in my early teens when I first expressed my desire to write music and be a Christian recording artist. Without warning, I found myself quickly being handed heaps of advice from all kinds of people— some I didn't even know! While the guidance of my family and my close friends was both insightful and invaluable, others left me with some "tips to think about" that I wasn't quite sure what to do with.

> God has not called us to do what seems possible, reasonable or normally attainable...We're supposed to be doing what is impossible and outrageous.
>
> —*GRAHAM COOKE*

As I approached my junior year of high school, I started to look at colleges and how I was to go about living this crazy dream that God had placed inside of me. When I told people about my desire to be involved in ministry, write songs, record music, and travel, I heard things like, "That's great, Paige! But just be sure to have a plan B... you know, just in case those things don't work out. You have to earn a living somehow, and sometimes what we want to do isn't always practical!"

Yes, I know there is certainly truth in that. I can't decide to live in a tree house and expect my food and money to sprout from the ground beneath me. Let's be real! But when I am talking about dreams and passions that I know God has led me to, isn't it a *lack of faith* to plan to be a banker just in case He doesn't come through?

The truth is, if we even so much as create a plan B for ourselves, that is what we will end up doing. Why? Because we gave ourselves a way to opt out. At the very moment when pursuing our true dream and calling becomes difficult and hard (and it will be at times!), Plan B safely waits in the sidelines, hoping that we will one day resort to its comfortable route.

Take heart. If you are currently not where you want to be, whether you are waiting on God's timing or are caught in a detour you feel He has brought you to, be encouraged. You are on the right path! If you have not given up on what He's called you to and are continually praying about where and what He would like you to do next, you are exactly where He wants you. You are being prepared and molded for what God is about to bring you. Don't be discouraged. If you are seeking Him, He will show up. He always does. (See Jeremiah 29:13 and Isaiah 41:13!)

> Are gamblers for gold so many and gamblers for God so few?
>
> —*C.T. STUDD*

When we wholeheartedly give ourselves to the radical plan that God has for us, the sometimes painful but always lovely path will certainly not look the way we thought it would. There are always twists and turns that we never would have chosen, but the outcome is far greater than we ever could have dreamed.

Are You Willing to Take the Risk?

There are people who do crazy things in the name of love, sports teams, spring break, and even a laugh…but what will *you* do in the name of our Lord Jesus Christ? How much will you allow your soul to be awakened?

Before I would sprint out the door, my mom used to tell me to take a jacket in case it got cool because "it's better to be safe than sorry." While she was certainly right concerning the jacket, think how crippling that phrase can be when we live our lives that way. The only way that we will be sorry in the end is if we miss out on the incredible adventure of fulfilling our purpose. Are you willing to lay aside the practical, normal, or even logical route that the world pulls you toward to reclaim the fire in your soul?

You and I have this mist of time on earth, and an eternity to think about what we did with it.

ACTION CHALLENGE

Talk to God every day for the next week about your biggest, wildest dream. Tell Him *what* you'd love to do, *why*, and your ideas of *how*. Ask Him every time you pray whether or not this is His dream for you, and if so, what He wants you to do about it. Be alert for creative ways that He will speak to you. Is He confirming what you have in your heart or leading you in another direction? Listen closely. His answer is the most important part.

10

LET THE FLAMES BEGIN

Has anyone ever flat-out asked you the question "What do you want to do with your life?" If so, chances are you did one of these three things:

(a) confidently explained your mapped-out future plans.

(b) said you had some ideas, but still were figuring out the details.

(c) freaked out and ran.

Which one sounds the most probable?

While you may now have an idea of your gifts and know that you definitely don't want to live a mediocre life...well, where do you go from here? With all of the options of what you could do still staring at you, how do you go about choosing?

Astronauts, Indiana Jones, and No Math, Please

When I was little, I felt very sure of what I wanted to be when I grew up. I had made up my mind. I was set on being an astronaut. I've always been fascinated by the sky and space, so, I figured, what would be better than to explore it myself?

As time went on my love for space remained, but I found some new interests that diverted my attention. Somehow, I took up the hobby of collecting rocks. I was obsessed. Anytime I left the house I could barely keep my eyes off of the ground for fear of missing *the coolest rock ever*! Soon after, my family moved into a farmhouse whose yard was full of all kinds of buried treasures. Sure, those "treasures" were broken pieces of pots and old tools, but to me, they were full of possibility. The stories behind each artifact—what it could have been or who it belonged to—intrigued me. I imagined the wildest stories of how they were used and what their owners' lives must have been like. This fascination led me to the conclusion that I wanted to be an archeologist who would uncover ancient buried cities and go on an endless variety of thrilling adventures. You know, Indiana Jones style.

When I was around ten, I decided I wanted to be a professional performer who would dance, sing, and act. A year later when I was diagnosed with cancer, those dreams seemed as good as gone. When the doctors told me that I wouldn't be able to dance like I used to because of my leg surgeries, I was heartbroken. I felt like my abilities, hopes, and practically everything had been taken from me. But while God closed one door, He opened so many more. God began to shape my heart and desires, giving me more specific dreams for what He wanted me to be. He began to show me that what mattered most was the passion He placed inside me, not the occupation I was set on choosing.

I've talked to countless friends, who, by the time they hit college, are completely at a loss for picking a major. They scan through all the different choices, ruling out a few that they definitely know they don't want to do (for me, math!), but they certainly can't narrow down the rest.

My good friend in high school was two years older than me, and I remember having many conversations about the whole college choosing process with him. He used to hate the perpetual questions that everyone asked his senior year…

"Well, Dan, where are you going to college? What are you going to do after you graduate?"

"Uhhh…" he thought, "I barely know where to begin!"

Though the enormous number of options before us truly *are* a gift, with every occupation swimming through our minds and the world running us every which way, it's easy to feel overwhelmed and left in the whirlwind of confusion. Even if you've thought thoroughly about what you want to do, I'm sure, like most of us, you've gotten dizzy imagining the various outcomes. Whether or not you started with about ten different crazy dreams like I did, we've all reached points where we question the true direction that we should go.

The Missing Piece

If you feel lost in the confusion and drowned in possibilities... *breathe.*

I have a proposition for you. What if your overall life decision were actually a lot less complicated than you think? Would you believe me if I told you that what we're really called to do is actually very simple?

As Christians, we are all called to the same thing.

Confused?

Let me explain.

When Jesus was asked what is the most important thing we are to do, He gave a clear answer that is directed toward each one of us. First, He wants us to love God with all our heart, with all our soul, and with all our mind. And second, He wants us to love our neighbor as we love ourselves (Matthew 22:37-39).

That's it.

Everything that we do with our life is meant to hang on those two commands. That's what our lives are supposed to be about!

We are all called to this one thing and frankly, Jesus couldn't have made it more clear.

Perhaps where things get complicated is in knowing how specifically we are each to live this out. In the midst of all the choices and opportunities in front of us and all that we could and should do, that deep question remains: *Why?* How can we possibly begin to tackle choosing a career without knowing the motivation behind that choice? This is the missing piece to the puzzle.

It's called passion.

Passion is what fuels us. It's what drives us when situations and circumstances fail. It's what motivates us to perform far beyond what we ever think we could be capable of.

But somewhere along our quest to discover what we want to do with our lives we lose sight of this essential piece. Instead, our lives merely become about doing what is practical (remember that conveyor belt?). In other words, we take the easy classes and avoid the hard professors. We find the quickest route instead of the one that would take a few extra years. We follow the socially acceptable dream without even considering what our God-given passions might be. And there we have it, folks! A surefire route to a passionless, mediocre life.

> The structure that channels your personal gifts toward Kingdom purpose is your career. Your career is not defined by school grades, your salary aspirations, or by mere opportunity. Your career is a custom-crafted calling from God to serve Him and His designs in the world through a particular occupation.
>
> —LILA EMPSON

This is why we have to come alive to our dreams! God has given each one of us unique desires and motivations for a reason. It's through those inner aspirations that God intricately brings about His incredible will for us.

What we do with our lives gives us the significant chance to have a divine partnership with God and grasp our heart's deepest dreams. That's a true adventure!

Finding Your Passion

At this point some of you may be asking, "Okay, Paige…even if I dare to dream again, how on earth am I to find my passion? Is it supposed to appear one day while the rest just falls into place?"

Well, maybe. But first, let me share a brief story that just might help you find your answer. Hold on, because we're about to turn everything you've heard upside down!

My girlfriend Melody and I were out together a while back, sipping Starbucks and causally wandering about in the warm evening weather. Somehow, through our many different threads of conversation, we began talking about this mysterious topic of "purpose"—what it means to different people, and how we are to live it out.

In our conversation, Melody said something that really struck a chord with me. I haven't been able to shake it since. She told me not to think of what you want to do with your life in terms of what you love, but rather, what you hate. In other words, what is it in the world that appalls, hurts, and breaks you? For Melody, it's human trafficking and slavery. For me, it's the thought of people wasting their lives. Taking those things we hate, we can then find a way to live our lives in such a way that we can impact and change that injustice or situation.

Like my friend Dan knows, it's easy to be overwhelmed when someone asks, "What do you want to do with your life? What do you love?"

"Uh, well…what if I love a lot of things? What if there are a lot of things I could do? Then what?"

Stop for a second and seriously consider the question Melody asked me: What do you hate? What truly, utterly, appalls you?

Got it?

All right. Here's the cool part. Now flip it around.

What can you do to solve it? Change it? Abolish it?

Are any thoughts coming to mind?

The beautiful thing about discovering what you hate and how you can change it is that the discovery ultimately brings you around to doing what you love. God wants us to delight in living the purpose that He's given us, which is why our passion plays such a huge part!

Many of us need to redefine the idea of what we're supposed to do with our lives. The world has given us the twisted message that our lifestyles should be practical, comfortable, and fit in a nice little box tied up with the ribbon of success. That way it's safe and no one gets hurt. Ha…*clearly!* This lack of living is creating a generation of walking dead!

Ultimately, here it is: I hate the thought of people wasting their lives. So I'm going for it. I am going to do anything I possibly can with my life to show people why they should live theirs. My purpose is to help other people find their purpose. That's what motivates me to do what I do. It's my passion.

When it comes down to it, it's not about a job. It's not about what the world coins as success or even the norm. It's about a reason, a passion, a purpose for which you were handpicked and specifically placed on this earth to live out. Whether you believe it or not, God has an amazing, passionate, and fulfilling plan for your life. You have a choice to take it or leave it.

For now the question stands: What do you hate?

Your answer just might be worth giving your life to.

ACTION CHALLENGE

Take a moment to consider the things that you love. Then consider what you hate. Think about what it would take to turn your last answer around into something positive.

What do you love?

What do you hate?

What is it about this that makes you upset?

What do you think you could do to change it?

11

BECOMING A WORLD-CHANGER

Joan grew up as a peasant girl in eastern France. Being the daughter of a farmer, she spent time tending her father's herds and learning how to keep house. When she was only 12 years old she began having visions from God. He was calling her to recover her homeland from English domination and lead the French army in battles during the Hundred Years' War. This call on Joan's life was very uncharacteristic for a girl of her time, let alone a girl in her humble position. It couldn't have seemed more impossible. Though seemingly unfit and ill-equipped, Joan showed bravery and dedication to the vision God gave her. Leading her armies to victory over and over again, the battles she won paved the way for the crowning of Charles VII, King of France. In 1430 she was captured by the Burgundians, sold to the English, tried by an ecclesiastical court, and burned at the stake. She was only 19 years old. Though her death was tragic, her legacy lives on. She is recognized throughout the world as an extraordinary young heroine.

When William was a boy, he was small and sickly with poor eyesight. After the death of his father, his mother struggled to cope and he was sent to live with his aunt and uncle. Though school was initially uninteresting to him, he completed his education and went on to college, where he began to enjoy parties and an active social life. During this time, he embarked on a tour of Europe that transformed his spiritual life and led him to commit his life and work to the service of God. Not only did this conversion change his party-loving lifestyle, but it sparked in him a life-long passion and concern for reform. William went on to become a British politician, a philanthropist, and a leader of the movement to abolish the slave trade. He headed the parliamentary campaign against the British slave trade for 26 years until the passage of the Slave Trade Act 1807, which abolished the slave trade in the British Empire but didn't free any slaves still under the yoke. William never gave up fighting, always working for the *complete* abolition of slavery, and he ultimately helped to pass the Slavery Abolition Act of 1833. William's health had been failing during those later years, and he died just three days after hearing that the passage of the Act to which he had dedicated his life was assured.

William said, "So enormous, so dreadful, so irremediable did the [slave] trade's wickedness appear that my own mind was completely made up for abolition. Let the consequences be what they would: I from this time determined that I would never rest until I had effected its abolition."

Esther, a young Jewish girl, lived with her cousin Mordecai after the death of her mother and father. The king of her time was named Xerxes, and he issued a royal decree that the most beautiful young virgins in the land should be brought before him. From these virgins the king would choose his next queen. Being a lovely girl, Esther was chosen, among others, to be taken before the king. With God's anointing hand on her, Esther won the favor of King Xerxes and was crowned the Queen of Persia. Meanwhile Haman, an evil, scheming advisor of the king's, persuaded

Xerxes to approve an edict that ordered annihilation of the Jewish people throughout the whole kingdom. Since Esther was a Jew herself, she was beside herself with grief. Mordecai told Esther that he believed she had become queen "for such a time as this," and challenged her to go before the king to plead for her people. Esther prayed and fasted for three days as she sought the Lord on what He would have her do. She knew very well that anyone who came before the king uninvited would be put to death—unless he extended his golden scepter to that person. As Esther courageously went before the king, she found favor with him and won him over to save her people and overrule the edict of the Jew's destruction. This young lady has a whole book of the Bible written about her and the incredible things that God did through her.

Martin grew up as the middle child in his family in Atlanta, Georgia. Being a noticeably exceptional student, he skipped ninth and twelfth grades and entered college at the age of 15—without having formally graduated from high school. After finishing his education, he married a woman named Coretta and took on his first position as a Baptist minister. Martin also became a civil rights activist early in his career. As a member of the executive committee of the NAACP (National Association for the Advancement of Colored People), he accepted leadership of "the first great Negro nonviolent demonstration of contemporary times" in the United States.

During these days of peaceful protest, Martin was arrested, his home was bombed, and he was subjected to personal abuse. Yet in the midst of all this he emerged as a leader of the first rank. Martin traveled over six million miles and spoke over 2,500 times, appearing wherever there was injustice, protest, and action. At the age of 35, Martin was awarded the Nobel Peace Prize for his work to end racial segregation and discrimination through civil disobedience and other nonviolent means—the youngest man to have ever earned that distinction. But on April 4, 1968, Martin was assassinated in Memphis,

Tennessee. His work set the stage for more change to come, and his memory lives on as one of the greatest orators and champions of human rights in American history.

~

Born in 1910 in Macedonia, Agnes was the youngest child in her family. Her father died when she was eight years old, and her mother shouldered the burden of raising a family on her own. In her early years, Agnes became fascinated by stories of missionaries. By the age of 12, she had committed herself to a religious life. Agnes left home when she was 18 to join the Sisters of Loreto as a missionary, where she changed her name to Teresa. She served as a teacher at the Loreto convent school for almost 20 years, and in 1944 was appointed headmistress. Though Tersea enjoyed teaching, she became increasingly disturbed by the poverty surrounding her. The Bengal famine of 1943 had brought misery and death to the city, and the outbreak of Hindu and Muslim violence plunged the town into despair and horror. During this time, Teresa experienced what she later described as "the call within the call" while traveling by train to the Loreto convent for her annual retreat. As she later told the story, "I was to leave the convent and help the poor while living among them. It was an order. To fail would have been to break the faith."

For over 45 years Teresa ministered to the poor, sick, orphaned, and dying while guiding the Missionaries of Charity's expansion, first in India and then throughout the world. At the time of her death, Mother Teresa's organization operated 610 missions in 123 countries and included hospices, homes, soup kitchens, children's and family counseling programs, orphanages, and schools. She is known and loved throughout the world as one of the most compassionate people who has ever lived.

~

Joan of Arc, William Wilberforce, Queen Esther, Martin Luther King Jr., and Mother Teresa were world-changers. Each of them were undeniably different from the others, but there is one thing they hold in common—the very reason they changed the world.

They each had a mission.

At the heart of the radical lives they lived and the history-making ways they changed the world was a mission God had placed inside of them. It was only through their trust and obedience to His call that they were able to change the course of human history.

Super-Humans Only?

If you're like me, when you read biographies of people like this it's like you're reading about some sort of superhuman creature who was unrealistically radical in the way they lived. *If* these people were human, their stories had to be embellished or enhanced with special effects and extra drama to seem more heroic…right?

The exciting (yet somewhat uncomfortable) truth is that there is no difference between any of these people and *you*. Exciting because it means your potential is enormous. Uncomfortable because your life may seem anything but world-changing.

The miracles of these peoples' lives weren't accomplished by the individuals themselves, but by the God who enabled and called them. He did the history making. All they did was answer the call that He gave them. They all said *yes!*

The same God who spoke to Joan of Arc in a vision, who fought William Wilberforce's battles, who granted Esther the favor of the King, is calling you, equipping you, protecting you, and readying you to fight for the mission He has given you to change the world.

> Jesus Christ is the same yesterday and today and forever.
>
> —HEBREWS 13:8

The World-Changer in You

Inside of every one of us is the hidden desire to *be* significant and to *know* significance in our lives. While some of us would never admit that to anyone, even ourselves, deep down we long to be a part of something that makes a difference. There is a world-changer in the depths of all of us.

Jesus gave a charge to His disciples before He left the earth, and He gives it to each one of us as well. He says, "Go and make disciples of all nations, baptizing them in the name of the Father and of the Son and of the Holy Spirit, and teaching them to obey everything I have commanded you. And surely I am with you always, to the very end of the age" (Matthew 28:19-20). Notice that this verse does not start out by saying, "To those few who are called to a radical life." It just says *Go!*

This is our challenge and clue to the fact that we are all called to a life that is world-changing. How else can we "go and make disciples of all nations"?

So many of these famous heroes came from the most humble and even unlikeliest of places. Joan of Arc was a peasant. William Wilberforce was a scrawny, sickly child who never grew much beyond five feet or weighed more than 100 pounds. Esther was a poor orphan living with her cousin. Martin Luther King Jr. lived in a society that persecuted him and paid him little respect. Mother Teresa started her ministry on the streets with no home or money. But the rest of their stories are history. If God could do great things with them, perhaps there is hope for us too.

The only thing standing between most people and the world-changer they could be is understanding God's mission for them and saying *yes* to it. Have you ever considered that you have a mission? Do you have any idea what it could be? Proverbs 29:18 says, "Where there is no vision, the people perish" (KJV). It reminds us that without a clear picture of what we're meant to do, we can't go on living. Our hope is lost, our reason has vanished, and our purpose is left unaccomplished.

We *need* a mission.

The Heart of a Mission

A mission is a specific purpose that one is sent to complete.

Let's unpack that a little bit. Within the definition are three essentials:

1. Our mission is for a *specific purpose*.

2. We are *sent*.

3. It is meant to be *completed*.

A soldier sent on a special mission knows that there is a need and urgency to the task in front of him. Just like that soldier, there is also an urgency as we carry out *our* mission. Lives are at stake. History depends on it.

So how does God raise up this mission inside of us? Where does it come from?

At the heart of our mission is our passion.

As we talked about in the previous chapter, our passion can be found by searching for that which we hate the most, and asking God how we can turn it around. For some of you, what you hate may be influenced by an injustice—a traumatizing experience you've had and you want to make sure it never happens to anyone else. Maybe it's something that you don't have a personal connection to but always felt was wrong. Whatever it is, *that* is your passion. There is nothing better to give your life to than the one thing that sets you ablaze.

Our passion is the key ingredient to creating our own personal mission statement. It's at the very heart of what we're called to do. Consider some of our famous examples. What was their passion? William Wilberforce hated slavery. He loathed it, despised it, abhorred it. His mission was to defend and restore freedom for God's people. Mother Teresa hated the devastation of poverty. Her mission was to heal and protect the needy, and, in doing so, give them hope and life. Martin Luther King Jr. hated racial segregation and discrimination. His mission was to unify all races and wipe out all divisions that society had built up against each other.

Do you see how the mission that led these people to change the world was rooted in their passion?

I love what author and speaker Laurie Beth Jones says in her book *The Path*—"If your mission holds no personal passion, it is not your path."*

---

* Laurie Beth Jones, *The Path* (New York: Hyperion, 2001), 49.

The Birth of a Mission

There are two elements to creating your mission statement: your passion and how you desire to change it.

Your Passion. It's important to understand what the focus should be on. While we started with the question of what we hate, the point is to take what we believe is the root of that hatred and determine what needs to be in its place. Your passion is what you desire the thing you hate to become.

My friend Carrie hated terrorism. As we dug a little deeper, we realized that "terrorism" was not the root—it was only a byproduct. We found that what she really hated was injustice and the violation of God's truth, so her passion was for justice and God's truth.

This goes much deeper. When Carrie and I began the process of uncovering her mission, she felt scattered by everything she wanted to do. She'd gone to school for massage therapy but while starting her own practice, she also desired to be involved in foreign issues. Feeling confused by these seemingly extreme opposites, she had brushed them off as being separate and random. However, when we began to go through the process I'm about to share with you, we found that those seemingly random interests and passions *were* related—and that she was uniquely wired to bring them together.

Your How: This is the way that God has created you to change what you hate. This relates to your gifts and personality. Sometimes it's hard to pinpoint those things and put them into a one-sentence statement. So I want to lead you through an exercise that I found incredibly beneficial. In her book *The Path,* Laurie Beth Jones guides her readers through a list of verbs and has them choose the ones that excite them. I want to take you through a similar list as this method was eye-opening and led me to discover a surprising pattern in the words I selected.

Creating Your Mission Statement

Circle three words in each of the six sections that are the most meaningful to you. (You do not have to choose one word from each row—just three from each section that grab you.)

SECTION 1

Arrive	Ignite	Imagine
Spread	Amplify	Volunteer
Teach	Contribute	Compliment
Brighten	Appreciate	Inform
Achieve	Arise	Confirm
Adopt	Believe	Protect
Relieve	Finish	Connect
Affect	Dream	Reach
Show	Commit	Counsel
Affirm	Approach	Train
Honor	Compose	Build
Elect	Practice	Illuminate

SECTION 2

Create	Defend	Demonstrate
Serve	Rise	Guide
Donate	Delight	Administer
Determine	Deliver	Advise
Comfort	Devote	Discover
Reconcile	Encourage	Call
Discuss	Formulate	Embrace
Drive	Manage	Give
Enhance	Enroll	Enlighten
Resolve	Introduce	Command
Embolden	Bless	Engineer
Cause	Franchise	Profess

SECTION 3

Exalt	Restore	Heal
Facilitate	Evaluate	Finance
Energize	Influence	Calculate
Impassion	Explore	Further
Entertain	Submit	Sacrifice
Forgive	Mature	Hold
Negotiate	Claim	Inspire
Host	Incorporate	Include
Translate	Improve	Keep
Identify	Remind	Find
Soar	Improvise	Engage

SECTION 4

Know	Intercede	Pursue
Work	Launch	Lead
Win	Go	Open
Love	Cherish	Receive
Merge	Exclaim	Organize
Make	Illustrate	Mold
Validate	Gain	Participate
Light	Motivate	Express
Follow	Realize	Plan
Live	Guard	Reclaim
Trust	Move	Perform
Model	Nurture	Understand

SECTION 5

Nourish	Produce	Proclaim
Persuade	Share	Speak
Play	Progress	Carry
Oppose	Redeem	Reflect
Praise	Promise	Bind
Own	Breathe	Reform
Prepare	Stand	Esteem
Qualify	Promote	Relate
Present	Seek	Assemble
Free	Provide	Support
Communicate	Diminish	Reflect
Touch	Refine	Journey

SECTION 6

Relax	Charge	Warn
Tell	Resonate	Satisfy
Release	Discern	Think
Trust	Respect	Save
Remember	Offer	Utilize
Soothe	Wait	Worship
Renew	Return	Surrender
Team	Correct	Maintain
Choose	Use	Verbalize
Penetrate	Value	Write
Travel	Dare	Supply

Look over the verbs you have chosen and write them down on a separate piece of paper. Do you see a pattern? Is there a certain theme or similarity? We are each drawn to different words over others. What might stand out to me you may gloss over, and vice versa. This exercise reveals our built-in desires, and how we are wired to live out our passion.

Now, of all the words that you have circled, choose your overall top three and list them here:

1. _____

2. _____

3. _____

These are the three words that mean the very most to you and resonate in a special place in your heart. The three final verbs you have chosen are the *how* in living out your mission.

Complete this sentence and make it your own: **My mission is to (insert your three verbs) (insert your passion) in order/for/so that (what you hate).**

For example, here is mine: My mission is to inspire, ignite, and reclaim purpose in others, so that they will not waste their lives.

YOUR MISSION STATEMENT:

My mission is to...

Please feel free to play with the wording to make it your own. My "equation" is for guidance. The point is not to fit your life's purpose into a formula, but to have a mission statement that makes sense to you and excites you. Make it clear and memorable so that you can hold it in your heart and daily live it out.

What Your Mission Is and Isn't

Defining your mission is a big undertaking, but it's one of the most profound things you'll ever do.

Your mission is the platform that God has given you to build your life upon. Now, I in no way want to give the impression that our lives are based on any "platform" other than Christ. What I mean is that your mission is the root and heart of what you do. It's your reference for every decision; it's your reminder and confidence of what God has called you to.

Your mission is not a career choice. It is far bigger than that. The mission that God has given you is designed to be lived out in many different ways, not just in one job.

Your mission is not a replacement for God's direction. Scripture is clear when it comes to our purpose, and only the Lord can truly direct our steps. Our mission statement in no way removes our need to seek guidance from God. It simply gives us a reference point. Proverbs 16:9 says, "In their hearts humans plans their course, but the LORD establishes their steps."

My rule of thumb has become this: Write your mission in pen and your plans in pencil.

The Final Wave

While writing this chapter I've been staying at a condo in Florida that overlooks the ocean. My soon-to-be mother-in-law was kind enough to bring her daughter, Mandy, and me on a writing retreat. When I wake each morning, I walk outside my room to see the most breathtaking view of a blue-green ocean. I've spent a lot of time staring out into this beauty and finding myself captivated by the motion of the waves. They carry so many stories, so many metaphors, so much meaning.

When Mandy and I waded out waist-deep in the ocean, we'd be in the middle of a conversation when all of a sudden a big wave would sneak up behind us, crash down, and slap us in the face. We'd always come up laughing. It's funny how some waves hardly brushed us at all while others practically drowned us!

When I looked out at these waves up high from our balcony, I saw what was really happening. Some waves rise up in the distance, brewing far from shore. Other waves remain calm and hardly noticeable, but *those* waves stand above the rest. They foam in the distance, forewarning you of the power they'll have when they finally crash on the shore. They are coming fearlessly, relentlessly. They are unstoppable. When one of these waves rises up, the other waves seem to disappear. Their impact is suddenly lost and they go unnoticed when they reach the shore. But when that big wave finally crashes up on the beach, it touches everything. It roars its warning and sweeps so far and so wide that even people who didn't intend for their toes to get wet end up soaked.

Our lives are like these waves. There are countless waves that crash along the shore each day, but only some leave an impact. Either we blend in and get lost, or we rise above the norm for the powerful mission we've received.

So what kind of wave will your life be? Will you come and go with hardly a trace? Or will you allow God to sweep you up and give your life power that will leave the whole shoreline changed forever?

ACTION CHALLENGE

1. Share your mission statement with your family and close friends. Ask them to encourage you in living it out.

2. Pray over your mission each day. Ask the Lord to show you *how* He desires you to live the mission He's given you.

3. Write your mission statement down. Put it in a place where you will see it daily.

4. Smile and feel awesome. You hold the missing piece to being a world-changer...your very own mission!

12

NOT JUST DREAMS

My dad and I sat in O'Charley's, sipping our soup and picking at the soft rolls on the table. I was sure our waiter thought that I was rude and grumpy because I hardly looked at him when he came to the table. Let's just say my demeanor was less than amiable. My dad and I were there to have a "meeting." I had been in a funk about some things in my life and needed to sit down and talk them out. We had just moved to Nashville about a year before, and I still felt the pang of loneliness after leaving behind my hometown. I was also overwhelmed and confused by some big life decisions I was making. When I graduated high school the year before, I felt God calling me not to go to college right then, but rather to begin the ministry that He was giving me. Though God had led me to that path very specifically and clearly, at times I wrestled with the fact that it was different from the path most of my peers were taking. I felt like my mission made me an outsider to my own friends. I wasn't a college student, but I wasn't an independent adult either. I wasn't sure where I fit or which map I was supposed to follow.

After I unloaded my frustration on my dad, he asked me an interesting question. I'd heard it and asked it many times before, but this time I understood it in a different way. He asked, "Paige, what do you think God's will for you is?"

Stammering to collect my thoughts and wanting to be sure of what he meant, I replied, "You mean, His will for me *right now?*"

To which he said, "Well, what else is there?"

I sat for a second in silence.

Of course! What else *is* there? Regardless of all my plans and thoughts about what I was going to do "someday," God never promised me tomorrow. I was reminded again of James 4:14—"You are a mist that appears for a little while and then vanishes." Suddenly I felt silly for being so wrapped up in the future that I hardly considered what I was supposed to be doing now. Instead of focusing on carrying out my mission today, I was telling myself, "When I have enough of this—*then* I'll do that!"

All we have is today. Right now. I was putting off things I could be doing now for some distant future plan. I was waiting on time that wasn't promised to me.

Our Mission Starts Now

Now that we have our mission, it is important that we not wait to live it out. The idea that we need to get things together before taking action may swirl around our heads, keeping us from getting started. For you planners, perhaps you feel there is a list that you must check off before you begin. For those of you who are more go-with-the-flow, you may feel like you have plenty of time to act on your mission. You'll get around to it eventually, you think.

Whichever side you lean toward, take to heart that there is urgency in your calling. You have an unknown amount of time to live it out. As a young person, society tricks us into thinking that we have all the time in the world to get our lives together. This message couldn't be more dangerous, or more false. Why else do so many adults wake up in a midlife crisis, having been baited into believing that one day they would finally just get it all together? If they had only taken the time to get on the right track when they were younger, perhaps they would have been spared the wasted years, regrets, and despair.

When I began writing this book and looking for a publisher, one of the publishing houses that considered me came back with the conclusion that they would rather not publish a book by a twenty-something. They felt that I should wait until I was 40 to write a book. At that point, they said, I would have more experience to put behind the lessons I was teaching. While I certainly hope that by the time I'm 40 I'll have more wisdom and experience, does that mean I should neglect 20 years of sharing what God is teaching me? I know I am young, and I take pride *and* humility in that fact. Yet if I had taken their advice, you wouldn't be reading this book, and I would have missed out on the mission that God is calling me to live right now—today.

Five Ways to Begin

So what are we waiting for? It's time to turn our mission into action!

The mission statement you wrote in the last chapter is going to change lives. Not the statement itself, but the way you take the words and put them into motion. Though you may have no idea where to begin, it is God who equips you and opens doors. All you have to do is be willing to take the first step. All you have to do is say yes!

Here are five essential and tangible ways to get you started:

1. Write down your mission and goals.

Statistics show that people who write down their goals have an 80 percent higher success rate of achieving them. If this is the case, then perhaps there's something to be said about acknowledging our dreams and putting a pen to them! If you have written down your mission in the last chapter, then you have already completed the first part. I want to encourage you, however, to write it on a sticky note, card, notebook, or whatever comes to hand. Just make sure it's placed somewhere you will see it daily. This will encourage, guide, and remind you of the incredible purpose God gave you. It will help to keep you from losing sight of your path.

With your mission clearly in view, it is also important to write down every possible idea that comes to mind of how to concretely live it out. These are your goals. Don't even think about how crazy or seemingly unattainable they may be. You may just look back someday and be surprised at the dreams that came to fruition!

> There is a tide in the affairs
> of men,
> Which, taken at the flood,
> leads on to fortune;
> Omitted, all the voyage of
> their life
> Is bound in shallows and
> in miseries.
> On such a full sea are we
> now afloat;
> And we must take the cur-
> rent when it serves,
> Or lose our ventures.
>
> —WILLIAM SHAKESPEARE,
> Julius Caesar

I recently found a few journals in which I'd written down my mission, goals, and specific dreams as a teenager. I'm not sure what led me to write them down consistently, other than the fact that there was something tangible about writing down the deepest desires of my heart and who I wanted to be. Each year as I wrote them down and prayed over these dreams for guidance, I began to feel more confident in who God was calling me to be. Having a clear picture of my mission on paper made me more willing to take risks in stepping out into the unknown. And by the way...many of the big, crazy dreams that I wrote down have been or are being fulfilled now.

When God spoke to the prophet Habakkuk, He said, "Write this. Write what you see. Write it out in big block letters so that it can be read on the run. This vision-message is a witness pointing to what's coming. It aches for the coming—it can hardly wait! And it doesn't lie. If it seems slow in coming, wait. It's on its way. It will come right on time" (Habakkuk 2:2-3 MSG).

2. Learn everything you can about your mission and your passion.

Educate yourself on the things that have to do with your mission. Your job right now is to acquire knowledge and insight into your cause. Research the history, facts, and statistics behind your cause. Take courses. Interview people who are further along the path than you are and have already made a difference in that area. Get in on the action!

Consider what you know about your mission. Do you know what is currently going on in the world regarding that issue? Do you know who or what is helping to change it? What are some of the issue's most prevalent needs? It is so important that we saturate ourselves in anything and everything that has to do with the mission that God has given us. This knowledge will guide us specifically to what we can do to make an impact. Remember, "The one who gets wisdom loves life; the one who cherishes understanding will soon prosper" (Proverbs 19:8).

3. Decide on one mission-driven action that you will take today.

When brainstorming the ways that you can live out your mission, which of your ideas will you start with? Once you have accomplished your first goal, move on to the other items on your list. Living your mission is not about checking off lists, but pursuing a lifestyle of purpose. Sometimes, however, it helps to start by taking each goal one at a time to train ourselves to take bold steps in fulfilling our mission.

A good place to start is right where you are. Oftentimes, as we look for opportunities to take action on our mission, we don't have to look any further than our everyday circumstances. How can you live out your mission with the people immediately around you? Are there needs among your family, friends, or community that perhaps line up with your passion? *Start there.*

In one of the parables Jesus told, a master gave bags of gold to his servants. To the servants who invested the money wisely the master said, "Well done, good and faithful servant! You have been faithful with a few things; I will put you in charge of many things" (Matthew

25:21). Be faithful with the "little things" today, and watch how God uses your obedience in the future!

4. Examine your resources and make use of them.

More people and things surround you who can help you accomplish your mission than you realize. Perhaps your parents, teachers, friends, or church leaders have untapped knowledge and experience in the very things you are looking to do. Who do you know who is remotely involved in your passion? Decide whether he or she would be someone you could get together with for coffee. Use that time to pick their brain! It might surprise you how willingly they will meet with you, as your interest in their knowledge will intrigue and honor them. Share your mission and explain the ideas and goals you have. Ask if they have advice or resources to connect you with that could help you get started. Most likely, they will help you themselves or will know someone to put you in touch with. You'll be amazed at how inspiring this kind of networking can be. By the way, don't be intimidated to seek out someone who may seem way beyond your reach. If you respectfully share your mission and request their advice, who knows what interest they may take in you when they see your passion and desire to live out your call!

> The purposes of a man's heart are deep waters, but a man of understanding draws them out.
>
> —PROVERBS 20:5

You can continue your research with applicable books, events, groups, and Internet research. These are great sources for learning and connecting with the cause of your passion. Such insight and tremendous ideas can come from these. They will leave you inspired! As you go forward, remember that "Plans fail for lack of counsel, but with many advisers they succeed" (Proverbs 15:22).

5. Pray!

Have you ever been faced with a problem where your hands are tied? You might mutter, "I guess all I can do is pray."

Sometimes prayer is our last resort. It's a desperate, final attempt rather than our first. Prayer is often treated with an "if all else fails" mindset when in all reality, it's all we have. I always shake my head when I find myself handling problems this way. After I've tried everything else in my own strength and mumble a prayer to God for help, I understand the irony of saying "I guess all I can do is pray," when really, the *only* thing I can do is pray. What else do I have to offer without Him?

It is impossible to live our mission and the purpose of our lives if we are not in close communication with God. This is not *our* dream or plan to run along and do with as we please. Our mission is *from* the Lord and *for* the Lord. It doesn't even exist without Him.

One of my favorite verses in Psalms says, "Trust in him at all times, you people; pour out your hearts to him, for God is our refuge" (Psalm 62:8). Oftentimes we think

> Commit to the LORD whatever you do, and he will establish your plans.
> —*PROVERBS 16:3*

this kind of personal sharing—this "pouring our hearts out"—should only happen with a close friend or someone paid to listen, like a counselor. One of the beautiful things about prayer is that it should be our most intimate conversation. For once, we don't have to explain ourselves when we talk…He *knows!* We can be honest and real and truly ourselves. There is no one else we can share our burdens with who actually has the power to do something about them like He does. There is no one who cares about us and our heart's desire more than He does.

I used to wonder how God could hear my prayers while listening to everyone else's around the world. I thought about all the other prayers He was receiving and wondered if I should waste His time with my petty concerns. Yet somehow, in a way I can't begin to understand, He hears *all* of our prayers. Not a single one of them bounces off the ceiling or is put on hold until He has the time to notice. Our communication is unbelievably precious to Him and as essential as air for us.

> If you read history you will find that the Christians who did the most for the present world were precisely those who thought most of the next. It is since Christians have largely ceased to think of the other world that they have become so ineffective in this.
>
> —*C.S. LEWIS*

In all pressing situations there is but one solution: pray first and foremost, pray without ceasing. God will not put you off; that is not in His nature. In Luke 18:7 Jesus asks His followers, "Will not God bring about justice for his chosen ones, who cry out to him day and night?"

Prayer should always be the first item on our to-do list, but it should never be crossed off. Pray for your relationship with Him, that He would deepen it and draw you more in love with Him. Pray for wisdom and guidance in how He would have you live your mission. Ask Him to open the doors He wants for you and pray for boldness and courage to walk through them. Pray that He would equip you to impact others through your calling. Pray that they would be rescued, changed, freed, and healed. Pray for God's will for them and for yourself. Lay yourself down at His feet…surrendering your dreams, your heart, and your very life. Let your prayer always be, "Here I am. Send me!" (Isaiah 6:8).

The Dream of Your Mission

What keeps a person's mission alive is the vision and hope that they have for it.

This is what excites them and keeps them pressing on when circumstances feel grim. Our dream for our mission should be clear in our minds and unadulterated by physical limitations and personal cynicism. With God *all* things are possible (Matthew 19:26, Philippians 4:13), and when we limit the hope of our mission, our doubt shrinks our possibilities and the scope of God's ability to work through us.

In light of this…think ginormous! Throw off "realities" that can string you up and let yourself drift into the free, unlimited potential of where your mission could take you and how the world could be changed by it. Take a few minutes to prayerfully consider these four questions:

What do you want to do in life more than anything else?

What would you do if you had no limitations?

If you could change the world in one way, what would that be?

What great event or change would you like to witness taking place in your lifetime?

Your Legacy

If you've ever read the book of Ecclesiastes in the Bible, it is pretty clear what Solomon, the wisest, richest man who ever lived, thinks of our life on earth and the physical, material things that we put stock in: *Meaningless.*

This word, *meaningless* (or *vanity* in some translations) appears 37 times in Ecclesiastes. The wisdom that God gave Solomon allowed him to see past all of the wealth and pleasures of the world and into the reality behind them. Everything that his hands could hold would perish. Only what is unseen lasts…yet how difficult it is to wrap our minds around that thought!

> So we fix our eyes not on what is seen, but on what is unseen, since what is seen is temporary, but what is unseen is eternal.
>
> —*2 CORINTHIANS 4:18*

Of all the things that fade on this earth, our legacy remains. Have you ever thought about the kind of legacy you want to leave? *This* is what will follow you into eternity. Take some time to reflect on and answer these questions about your legacy.

What would you most like to be known for?

What three qualities would you most like to have associated with your name?

How do you want to be remembered?

How do you want the world to be different because of how you've affected it?

What do you want the Lord to say of you when you finally step into His presence in Heaven?

ACTION CHALLENGE

You can start leaving your legacy by living it daily. Consider the answers that you wrote down to the questions in this chapter and examine whether or not you are currently living out these qualities and goals. If not, start now.

13

"OH, SNAP!"
MOMENTS

Brianna grew up in a small town where she went to a Christian school before starting homeschool in fourth grade. She was the quiet one, more of an observer, who preferred not to raise her hand in class where attention would be drawn to her. Speeches, sports, or anything that meant eyes would be on her were out of the question.

But when Brianna was 15, her life took a turn that she'll never forget. At the time, she was questioning her relationship with God and wondering what she was missing that would make that relationship more personal. "I was the little kid who kept saying 'the prayer' over and over again, just to make sure I did it right," she said. "But I wanted more than a Sunday school relationship with Him…I knew it could be intimate and real, and I was hungry for that." This desire was the beginning of Brianna's quest to know God, to seek His face and what He desired for her life. As she sought Him, she underwent a journey to understand who she was, what her views on life issues were, and what she truly believed in. Her desire to know the Lord simultaneously unveiled her true self.

One of the things she discovered was that she was passionate about abstinence and purity. These were two things she felt mattered and made a difference. As she began to embrace this passion, she tried to surround herself with people and involve herself in events that would help her grow in this area. When she heard that the True Love Waits rally was coming to a nearby city, she knew she had to be there. One of her friends, who headed a crisis pregnancy center and often spoke on the radio, suggested to the station that they interview Brianna about the rally she was going to. In essence, she could be the "reporter" from the event and share the message of purity with the station's listeners. When Brianna got an unexpected call from the head DJ of the station, she was sure they had the wrong number. Quickly reassuring Brianna that they were looking for her, the DJ asked if she could give a 20-minute interview on the morning show so listeners could gain insight from the rally. Even though accepting went completely against her shy personality and *everything* in her screamed, "Hang up the phone!" she felt the Lord tugging her heart to do the very thing she feared most. "Getting in front of a microphone and being asked a bunch of questions was the last thing I wanted to do!" she explained. "Yet it was one of those moments where even though I was scared, my stomach was turning, and the easy thing to do would have been to say no…I knew this could help someone, and if I don't talk about it, who will? I was going to that event to be encouraged by people who were willing to stand up and talk about it, so how could I not do the same?"

So she said yes and hung up the phone…and then freaked out. But when the morning of the interview finally came, the 20 minutes that the DJ originally planned turned into *two hours!* The conversation went so well that they started to take calls. Brianna had to answer live listener questions! Though she was shaking and scared to death, she felt the Lord speak through her and give her exactly what she needed to make it through.

Brianna thought that she had survived a one-time radio experience, having no idea what God had planned for her next. She was soon called back to do *another* interview, and after that the station asked if she would be willing to be the new weekend DJ.

Surely this time they were joking—she was only 15! There was no way she could even respond to such a silly suggestion. But again, they were serious. She had another decision before her. She tried not to panic.

"I knew it was easier not to do it," she said. "God's not going to be mad at me if I don't, but *I'm* going to miss out on a lot. I'm going to miss out on this roller coaster adventure that He has for me. In my heart, I knew God was calling me to do it. Ultimately, I wanted to be faithful."

The first day that Brianna went in to be the weekend DJ, it took her ten minutes to even test the mic. She recalls, "I didn't want the DJ setting me up to hear my voice. *I* didn't even want to hear my voice! I kept thinking, 'This is proof that you're crazy for asking me to do this— I can't even test the volume!'"

Brianna found her strength in writing Bible verses and the lyrics of worship songs in her notebook and staring at them before she would go on the air. It was her way of reminding herself who God was, and, she says, that was the only way she was able to do it.

As she was faithful each week, the station began to receive input from listeners. The audience loved the new DJ and were really inspired by her program. Brianna's goal was to make the airtime matter. She wanted to encourage people. She decided that if this was where she needed to be and how she was supposed to spend her time, it *had* to matter. Otherwise, it was a waste! She certainly didn't want to do this for herself, and she wouldn't have kept going in her own strength. She kept going by hanging on to the promise that God had a plan, and He knew what He was doing.

Soon her role as the weekend DJ expanded to stepping out of the enclosed studio and onto live stages at concerts where she was expected to represent the station. This was a new terror of unknown proportions! "I *had* to get on my knees," she told me. "I had to say 'God, you have to help me talk to these people!' It was absolutely essential for me to have that alone time with Him, because that's what would build me up to be able to walk out there."

Besides being faced with the fear of getting up on stage, Brianna had the added pressure of being young. The DJs from other stations were all adult professionals…cool as cucumbers, trained, good speakers, and confident in their roles. Knowing that she came across as older on air, Brianna worried that perhaps people would shrug her off when they met her in person and saw how young she was. Her biggest fear was that people would disregard her and her work because of her age. "I didn't want them to dismiss me as 'just a kid,' or think that because I was young I didn't know what I was talking about. So much of my nervousness centered on the fact that I didn't think I was qualified. Ultimately, that wasn't at all true."

The truth was, God was using her right there at the age that she was! Her qualification didn't come from training or maturity. It came from the Lord, who brought her that opportunity and equipped her with the wisdom and strength that she needed. Brianna had little confidence on her own, but she had confidence in Christ, who enabled her to step out into the unexpected.

The wild journey with the radio station continued, and in a short matter of time Brianna was offered a job working at another station. She took the job and was quickly promoted to the main DJ position— live on the air during the popular late-afternoon drive time slot. "The only way I had enough strength was because God gave it to me every day. And it was never far in advance! It was *as* I was pushing the record button. Right when I needed it. I would prefer to have that strength hours in advance so I'd know for sure I'm going to be okay…but it doesn't work that way!"

When Brianna was 17, she felt God leading her away from her work with the radio and into a new phase of booking and promoting Christian concerts. When I asked her what she thinks she would have missed had she never stepped into this adventure with radio, she said, "Had I not done it, I don't even know where I'd be right now. Those little choices that I made when I was 15 and 16 years old started me on this journey that has directly affected where I am currently as a 23-year-old. God was stretching me and getting me out of my comfort zone, not to mention introducing me to people who have impacted my life forever."

Though at the time she couldn't imagine why God was bringing these opportunities when she was so young, she believes there was a reason that He brought them *then*. The impact can't be told of what she and countless others would have missed had she never set foot on the unknown path where He was leading her.

Facing the Uncomfortable

Just like Brianna, sometimes the things God calls us to do are out of our comfort zones. Though our mission is something we are passionate about and created to do, it will lead us into places we'd never thought we'd go.

I call those terrifying moments, when we're dragged kicking and screaming out of our safety nets, "Oh, snap!" moments. These are the moments when you know you can't do something on your own, but you bravely step out in faith anyway. Have you ever had one of those? Can you think of the way that you felt when you were faced with it?

There is nothing like the feeling of doing the impossible. That is why our "Oh, snap!" moments are some of the most amazing experiences that we can have. There is an obvious catch, though—we *cannot* get through them on our own!

The moment that I step on stage is always a *huge* "Oh, snap!" moment for me. I sang my first solo in front of an audience when I was four years old, and I was probably less nervous then than I am now! Any time that I get up in front of people to sing or speak, no matter how large or small the crowd, I get so nervous that I practically get sick. This is coming from the girl who's not only been on stage since she was four, but has been all over the country on TV and radio shows, speaking and singing on tour. How does *that* work?

Sometimes I've wondered why God would call me to do something that truly scares me to death. I've tried to reason with Him, saying it couldn't make sense to ask me to do something that makes me this nervous! Yet somehow, in a way that only God could come up with, He's proven that this is exactly what He has called me to…and given me peace about it! I've come to realize that singing and speaking is the one thing that brings me to the place where I am desperately dependent on God. Besides traumatic and unexpected crises, there is nothing else I face that brings me to my knees in this way. I can't walk out on that stage by myself. There is nothing that I have to say or offer if God doesn't guide my words, bring peace to my composure, and give me strength for every step. The amazing thing is that even though inwardly I am shaking like a leaf, for years now, people have come up to me after events to say how impressed they were by my "calm and poised presence" on stage. Ha! *That wasn't me.*

The feeling of supernatural power that comes over me when I step out in that terrifying moment is truly surreal. Words, actions, and even confidence flow out of me that truly aren't my own. The biggest blessing is walking off that stage and knowing that the Lord just performed a miracle. Nothing brings me more joy or overwhelming satisfaction than being used by Him in that way.

When Jesus departed back to heaven, He promised that a Helper would come in His place. That Helper was the Holy Spirit. This Helper, He said, would do wondrous things through us if we did them in Jesus's name. "Peace I leave with you; my peace I give you. I do not give to you as the world gives. Do not let your hearts be troubled and do not be afraid" (John 14:27).

If Our Mission Were Comfortable...

When confronted with an "Oh, snap!" moment, many people will choose to opt out. "It's too hard." "It's scary." "It's inconvenient." These are all excuses people make for why they can quietly walk away from the Kingdom-building opportunity God is putting in front of them. Perhaps if they had stopped and realized all that they'd be *missing* by opting out, they might have reconsidered.

What if our mission were comfortable?

If our mission were comfortable there'd be no adventure. Let's face it. Who wants to watch a movie without some sort of exciting twist or adventure? There is always a hurdle to overcome or a battle to fight in every story that's worth watching. The best things in life aren't handed to us casually. A life of impact is attained through sacrifice, risk-taking, and fierce dedication. This kind of living cannot and will not lead you down a dull path. Just as the view from a mountaintop is enjoyed only by the person who climbs it, so is overwhelming joy and fulfillment awarded to those who endure for it.

If our mission were comfortable there'd be no growth. My friend Leah's mom used to say, "God never promised that being a Christian would be easy. He just said He'd get us through it." It's a harsh truth, but there's incredible comfort in it. Scripture actually says that this life *will* be tough! However, all throughout the Bible we are also told that our trials will bring about abundant blessings and extraordinary personal growth. We are reassured that though we will experience hardship, "our light and momentary troubles are achieving for us an eternal glory that far outweighs them all" (2 Corinthians 4:17).

The book of James tells us to consider our trials *pure joy* because the testing of our faith develops perseverance. The growth that happens when we are taken out of our comfort zones and brought through hard times is incomparable. Nothing can teach us or refine our hearts better than challenge. This growth is one of the greatest gifts that we can receive. Through it, Scripture promises, we will become "mature and complete, not lacking anything" (James 1:4).

If our mission were comfortable we wouldn't need God. When a little child discovers the new and glorious wonders of crawling, she no longer thinks she needs her parents' help. Her fledgling ability to move from one end of the room to another is the most brilliant advancement she believes she could accomplish! She can do it on her own and with some practice, it becomes comfortable. When her mom or dad begins to suggest the idea of walking by holding up her hands and guiding her little feet along, the baby collapses on the floor and goes right back to her crawling position. Why bother with this new and strenuous activity when she is perfectly capable of squirming around on her own?

Oftentimes we are like this with God. When we find a way of living that gets us by, we get comfortable. We settle in and scoff at any idea of doing what God may be suggesting. Little do we know we are crawling around on our stomachs when we could be walking.

If our mission were comfortable we'd have no power. If you and I operate comfortably on our own in everyday life, we will never see miracles. God wants to do something brilliant, huge, and unimaginable through us—but if we settle for what our small little hands can do, what an unspeakable loss! Jesus says, "If you remain in me and I in you, you will bear much fruit; apart from me you can do nothing" (John 15:5).

If our mission were comfortable we would be blind. Each one of us has a little bubble that we like to live within. Inside are all of our favorite items that we enjoy surrounding ourselves with. The strange thing is that although other people can see us through this bubble, we can't see them. The only way that we can see outside of this little blob that we've encased ourselves in is to step outside of it.

When we are stuck in our comfortable way of life we are blind to the world around us. We are blind to needs, problems, ideas, truth, and people. Most tragically, we are blind to the way that God desires to use us to impact the world.

Let's Get Messy

When I was diagnosed with cancer, the character of my friends was put to the test. They were faced with a difficult situation to handle. Their friend, who had previously been just like them, now looked different and was experiencing things that were hard to relate to. While some friends came even closer by my side, others sent cards from a distance. My friend Jill's response surprised me. While others stepped awkwardly away, she stepped in and got to know my needs, my pain, my condition. She learned what the hospital was like and what I had to do on a regular basis. I explained to her that there really wasn't a lot to do in the hospital. Most of the patients had to stay confined to their rooms watching TV all day, and that gets old after...a day.

When I had finished my last treatment and been "released into life," Jill threw me the first surprise party I ever had. I thought I was going to *her* party when it turned out to be a "Welcome Back" party for me! Sometime later she told me about an idea she had to start a group that would go to children's hospitals and perform special shows for the patients there. Jill and I knew each other through a theater arts program, so not only did we have a bunch of talented friends, we had all the songs and dance skills to do it! She formed the group and named it Kids4Kids. Jill chose the songs and directed them with full choreography, which we rehearsed and completed with costumes! It was a hit.

We took our shows to the local children's hospitals in our city and the surrounding area, and shared some of the most rewarding experiences with the young patients there. Most children would be rolled in wheelchairs from their rooms down into the area where we'd do our show. All of them had tubes and other objects (that were foreign to my friends) connected to their bodies as part of their treatment. It was an overwhelming sight to take in, but Jill and my friends only let that make them more determined to put a smile on the children's faces.

Jill stepped into a potentially uncomfortable situation, but knew the need was too great for that to stand in her way. Because she ventured out of her comfort zone, she was able to touch lives and bring joy to faces in desperate need of a smile.

Jill's story is the perfect example of how we have to be willing to get our hands dirty. For some of us, it may be incredibly uncomfortable to go to a hospital and interact with sick or hurting people. For others, it may be hard to talk with a homeless person on the street. Whatever our idea of uncomfortable or messy, we have to be willing to see the need beyond it and not let our pride stand in the way.

When I read about Jesus's life in the Gospels, I am always blown away not only by how God, the King of Kings, humbled Himself to be made into the form of a man, but how He always went to the rejects. He sought out the most despised, the ugliest, the smelliest, the most unwanted people, and went by their side, talked with them, and touched them with healing. He stepped into their mess and transformed the world.

The norms of our society—the things that don't make us bat an eye—are the very things that Jesus couldn't stand. Arrogance. Greed.

Hypocrisy. How ironic that we see these things every day on the news and in our own hearts, but we'll cross to the other side of the street to avoid the people Jesus would have embraced.

Maybe it's time we took a good look at what makes us uneasy... and why.

What Are We Afraid Of?

We all have a line. It's the line we've drawn between what we think is possible for us and what we'll never even attempt. Though we may have convinced ourselves that we have a whole list of reasons why we shouldn't do something, there is only one thing that truly holds us back. *Fear.*

When Peter was with the other disciples in a boat, they saw Jesus walking toward them on the water. At first they were terrified, thinking He was a ghost, but Jesus reassured them it was Him. Peter, still not sure that it was truly Jesus, said, "Lord, if it's you, tell me to come to you on the water" (Matthew 14:28). Jesus told him to come, so Peter stepped out of the boat and began to walk on the waves. (Talk about an "oh, snap!" moment!) Suddenly the wind picked up and Peter became frightened. In his fear, he began to sink. Jesus reached out His hand and caught him, saying, "You of little faith, why did you doubt?" (verse 31). Peter had been doing the impossible—he was walking on water! Yet while he was in the middle of this unbelievable experience, he let the wind stop him. This story is such a vivid picture of what fear does. The very moment Peter begins to fear, he starts to sink. It's a direct correlation.

Our fear can keep us from living out the mission to which we are called. There are four fears that stand in our way:

1. Fear of the unknown. It's human nature to want to know what is going to happen next. We feel completely lost and out of control when we can't predict how a certain situation will turn out.

In kindergarten, I remember our teacher conducting an experiment with wooden boxes that had a rubber opening at the top where you would insert your hand. The point was to blindly reach inside, feel whatever the box held, and guess what it was. I recall being *so* afraid to put my hand inside because I had no clue what my fingers would find! One box contained a snakeskin (which really freaked me out) and another held something soft and fuzzy. Though they were all perfectly safe objects, I reacted as though I expected to find a snapping alligator! It was kindergarten—I'm pretty sure I had nothing to fear. Yet the unknown still terrified me.

When we step where we cannot see, we feel as though we are standing naked in front of a crowd. We have no idea what we are exposed to, how we appear, or what's going to happen next. Our vulnerability unnerves us.

Yet to the God we serve, time is like a horizon stretched before Him. He sees its beginning and its end. There is no part that is hidden or out of His sight. There is no unknown. Though you and I can only see the moment that we're in, He sees the rest of our story. He is guiding us to certain places because He knows it will turn out amazing in the end. What is there to fear when the One who sees it all guides you with His hand?

2. Fear of failure. This is a big one for most people. It's the very reason that most dreams end up in the trash. That haunting question—what if?—can be suicide. What if this doesn't work? What if I can't do it? What if I fail?

Well, *what if* I told you that some of the world's most well-known, influential, and respected people failed at some point? When screen legend Fred Astaire went for his first audition, he received the following assessment from an MGM executive: "Can't act. Slightly bald. Can dance a little." NBA superstar Michael Jordan was once cut from his high school basketball team. Walt Disney was fired from a newspaper because he "lacked ideas." He went bankrupt several times before he built Disneyland. Bestselling author Max Lucado had his first book rejected by 14 publishers before finding one who would give him a chance. And as a young boy, Thomas Edison was told by his teachers that he was "too stupid to learn anything." Work was no better, as he was fired from his first two jobs for not being productive enough. And before succeeding at creating a working lightbulb, he created 1,000 lightbulbs that didn't work at all!

What if they had just given up? What if they had never even tried?

Failure is nothing to fear in itself. It's only our pride that makes it seem like the enemy. The only enemy you should fight is the one trying to keep you from the mission that God is calling you to. You and I may fall, but we can never truly fail. Not if we belong to the Lord Jesus Christ. Scripture says, "No, in all these things we are more than conquerors through him who loved us" (Romans 8:37).

3. Fear of rejection. Just like you saw in the examples above, rejection is first of all subjective. Don't you think the newspaper executive who fired Walt Disney for "lack of ideas" was kicking himself later on? There may be people in your path who completely reject your ideas, your mission, even you. This could be someone who's opinion you couldn't care less about, or someone you deeply respect. It is important that you use discernment when listening to suggestions. While God sends some to encourage you, Satan sends other to derail you.

When you choose to act upon the call God gave you, don't do it for the acceptance or approval of anyone. This is *your* mission to live out the purpose that God has entrusted to you. When you walk into it with this mindset, no rejection from man can stop you. "If God is for us, who can be against us?" (Romans 8:31).

4. Fear of pain. This is the fear that causes us to stay in our bubbles and play it safe. Many of us would prefer to avoid the paths we know are challenging. For instance, if someone desires a profession for which they'd need several extra years of schooling and must then work up to the position they'd like to have, they may shoot down the idea altogether before they even get started. It just sounds too time-consuming. Someone else may desire to be a missionary in a country that persecutes Christians, where sharing the gospel is incredibly dangerous. They may let fear cause them to reconsider, as they know they'd be risking their life.

Though our fear of pain and hardship is understandable, it's not acceptable when it comes to living out our mission. It's a cop-out. This is where we need to gather our strength and courage from the Lord and trust that, with Him, we can face whatever comes our way. Jesus *died* for us. Living for Him is the least we can do.

The Reason You Can Risk

Here's the thing. Though venturing out to fulfill your mission is a risk, it's not risky. You have nothing to lose!

Christians get to live life with the freedom and the power to do the impossible. We don't have to wobble into a situation, wondering if we're going to sink, because we know Christ's victorious arms have promised to sustain us! When we step out into the unknown, we step into *faith*. And faith is "confidence in what we hope for and assurance about what we do not see" (Hebrews 11:1).

To the person who lacks faith, this verse sounds nuts. The words *confidence* and *hope* don't normally go together, and neither do *assurance* and *do not see*. But this is why those who have experienced the living God believe they can do great things through Christ. They are not stepping onto rolling waves of uncertainty; they are stepping onto the firmness of their faith.

We are like little children standing with our toes curled over the edge of the pool. We can't swim, but we know that when we jump into the water our dad is going to catch us. Just like our Heavenly Father, He is standing there with His arms outstretched, waiting for us to jump.

Close your eyes and take a leap.

I dare you.

ACTION CHALLENGE

1. Pray for God to bring you an opportunity that takes you out of your comfort zone for His glory. Ask for open eyes to see it and the courage to move forward. Step into your "oh, snap!" moment and prepare to witness a miracle.

2. Think big—get others involved. Once you have stepped out of your comfort zone and experienced its effect, share the story with your friends and see if they'll join you. Whether it's coming alongside you in an action or finding a mission of their own, encourage them to see what can happen when they step out in faith.

14

WALKING THE LINE

Several years ago I had a conversation with a friend where we discussed that age-old question asked of Christians: If God is such a loving God, why does He allow so many bad things to happen? We all know the question. Many of us have asked it ourselves.

My friend offered an interesting new twist to the question. First, he defined darkness: the absence of light. If the world is full of darkness, he said, and darkness is the absence of light...where is the light?

In Matthew 5:14-16 Jesus says, "You are the light of the world. A town built on a hill cannot be hidden. Neither do people light a lamp and put it under a bowl. Instead they put it on its stand, and it gives light to everyone in the house. In the same way, let your light shine before others, that they may see your good deeds and glorify your Father in heaven."

You and I are called to be the light. If the world's such a dark and hurting place, perhaps it's not because God doesn't care. Instead, where are the people that He's placed on this earth to be the light and carry out His purpose? Francis Chan ventured to say in his book *Crazy Love* that God has more of a right to ask *us* why so many people are starving!

Paul tells us in 2 Corinthians 4:6 that "God, who said 'Let light shine out of the darkness,' made his light shine in our hearts." If God gave us His light to shine in the world, what exactly are we doing with it?

A Separate Culture

A subculture has been created that is separate from society. It has its own stores, music, videos, t-shirts, books, breath mints, brands, businesses, and buildings. The people within this culture seem to be very content inside this separate-from-society world. However, the people outside of this culture don't get it. They stand on the outside peering in with confusion at the strange world, not knowing what is within. As the outsiders wonder what is going on in there, a curious chatter arises among them, starting rumors that create a sort of stereotype of this culture and its people. Some searching onlookers have tried to enter into this separate culture, but as soon as they set foot inside they felt strange, different, judged. Word spread quickly of this seemingly unaccepting society and many outsiders felt resentment and coldness toward them. It wasn't that the people of this culture didn't want visitors, but they had removed themselves so far from the world that they exhibited an appearance that was aloof, misunderstood, and uninviting.

This society is a picture of Christian culture. While founded on good intentions, it has become a subculture that many view as cut off from the world.

I once heard someone ask, "Why is there a Christian music industry instead of Christians being *in* the music industry?" The question puzzled me at first, but now, I realize that this person had a valid point. I'm in the Christian music industry myself, and I hear a lot of hype about "Christian celebrities" and "top Christian artists." But when I talk about these artists to a person outside the Christian culture, I get a lot of blank looks. They've often never heard of these people or even one of their songs. The separation between Christian and secular culture is almost complete. I know my heart, and I know the intentions of my friends who are Christian artists. Our heart is for the Lord and we want to reach *everyone* with our music. Yet we are automatically cut off from the main world because we are part of this separate culture.

Please don't hear me wrong. I support music, books, businesses, and everything with a Christian heart and message. I am thankful for them and know they are essential! However, something has gone badly wrong. Many of these truth-giving resources have become like light hidden under a bowl that the verse in Matthew describes. Their biblical intention to be different from the world has turned into being separate from and unknown to the world. This is not what we as Christians intend, but the truth of what has happened. Don't believe me? Ask most anyone who is not a believer what they know about Christian culture.

In, Not Of

When Jesus walked on this earth, He seemed to make a point of doing things that shocked people. One night when He was having dinner with the tax collectors, the Pharisees demanded to know why He was associating with sinners. Jesus simply told them, "It is not the healthy who need a doctor, but the sick" (Luke 5:31).

Jesus went out of His way to spend time with the people who needed Him the most. He didn't put a sign outside a building saying that He'd be in there all day preaching and healing if anyone wanted to come. He went to *them.*

One of the things that drew everyone to Jesus was how He was *in* the world…but never *of* it. He was in the midst of complete darkness, yet He was always the light.

While many Christians believe they are honoring the Lord with the way they hide from the world, they neglect to realize how they are shutting God's light off from it. While it is essential for Christians to have fellowship and resources to be built up by one another, we are meant to take the encouragement and light we receive to the darkest of places. What good are our church services if we don't carry the truth we learn out into the world?

The world doesn't need some put-on religion that hides in the walls of a church or throws pamphlets at passersby. They need you and me to live Christ in a real way, *in* the world.

The Fine Line

My friends Mike and Daniel Blackaby recently wrote a book called *When Worlds Collide*. In it, they describe how Christians typically live out their faith in one of three ways:*

Cave Dwellers: Christians who fear the world and seek to insulate themselves from it as much as possible.

Cave-Ins: Believers who accept the world's values and compromise their faith or abandon it altogether.

Colliders: Christians who remain true to their faith yet effectively engage the world and are used by God to change people's lives.

Cave dwellers and cave-ins are the ones who shut off God's light from the world. There are two sides to everything, and two extremes. While some hide from the world, others blend in with it. There is a fine, *fine* line between them.

Cave-ins think that Christians must look exactly like the world in order to influence it. This is a devastating and dangerous idea. How can you tell them apart from secular society? It's like the cave-ins have put their light on a dimmer, hoping they can sneak into the darkness without blinding or offending anyone. But worse than offending anyone, no one will even see their light.

In the world we live in, we are taught to shut our mouths when it comes to our faith. While some Christians let this keep them quiet, others use it as an excuse to live a worldly lifestyle. You don't have to go get drunk with friends at the bar to witness. You don't have to light yourself a cigarette in order to talk to someone on their smoke break. You don't have to date a nonbeliever to bring them to God. You don't have to watch a raunchy movie in order to spend time with someone. These are all situations where we can confuse what is wrong with a fabricated "witnessing opportunity."

My girlfriend Kate and I attended a church group a while back. While there, I got to know that she's a solid believer who seeks to honor God. Recently, she was invited to go to a bar with some of her old friends whom she hadn't seen in ages. Since these friends were part

---

* Mike Blackaby and Daniel Blackaby, *When Worlds Collide* (Nashville, TN: B&H Publishing Group, 2011), 22.

of her old partying lifestyle before she knew the Lord, she decided this could be a casual opportunity to see and talk to them about the change God had made in her life. While at the bar, she decided to have a drink with them while they caught up. Though she was responsible and carried herself differently, she still appeared to them like the "old Kate" merely by joining them for a drink in the place where they used to party. Her very presence there sent a message of approval to those friends and the lifestyle they were living. Kate quickly realized that this was not the setting where they would ask questions about her faith. In that situation, she didn't appear different.

In the World...Set Apart

The tricky thing is that although the Lord wants us to be out *in* the world, in the midst of unbelievers, He also calls us to be set apart. We are not to do as the world does or think as the world thinks.

Romans 12:1-2 says, "So here's what I want you to do, God helping you: Take your everyday, ordinary life—your sleeping, eating, going-to-work, and walking-around life—and place it before God as an offering. Embracing what God does for you is the best thing you can do for him. Don't become so well-adjusted to your culture that you fit into it without even thinking. Instead, fix your attention on God. You'll be changed from the inside out. Readily recognize what he wants from you, and quickly respond to it. Unlike the culture around you, always dragging you down to its level of immaturity, God brings the best out of you, develops well-formed maturity in you" (MSG).

> We do not draw people to Christ by loudly discrediting what they believe, by telling them how wrong they are and how right we are, but by showing them a light that is so lovely that they want with all their hearts to know the source of it.
>
> —*MADELEINE L'ENGLE*

The things that God asks are actually for our own good. Hiding from the world or blending into it seems easier than actually facing it.

But when we hide or blend in we don't benefit others, and we certainly don't benefit ourselves.

The line between being *in* the world but not *of* the world is a fine one, but it's the line we must walk. It is a narrow path, and we have to cling to the Lord's strength to stay on it. I want to encourage you with a few stories of people who are currently walking this line, who are stepping out into the darkness of the world in the set-apart armor of their faith.

Holly's Story

Holly and I met when I first moved to Nashville. We were both from Pennsylvania, but our families moved to Tennessee where we had to start a new life and make new friends. We became close during our senior year of high school. She was my first friend in the area, and I was thankful to have her. When college season came around, she went out West to a school where she had received a great academic scholarship. Holly is a Christian, but the school she's going to is not. Having been homeschooled, she knew when she left for college that the experience would be unlike any she had ever had. When she first got there, she only met one other Christian. This girl happened to be a "Cave Dweller," and Holly quickly realized she didn't have much in common with her. The rest of the girls on her floor were pretty wild compared to what Holly was used to, and she realized that there were a lot of boundaries she'd have to set. She wanted to be careful, however, not to cut herself off but to befriend the girls even though they had very different morals. While Holly made a point of hanging out with them, she also made a point of watching what she did.

As she began to walk the line of kindly saying no to this and yes to that, she found the girls questioning why she lived differently. Having opened the door of communication by being their friend while staying true to who she was, she explained that she was a Christian and God cared about how she spent her time. God cared, she said, about underage drinking, hooking up with guys, dressing promiscuously, and using foul language. She shared about what God had done in her life and how she wanted to honor Him. Though the girls didn't quite understand, they grew to respect Holly for the decision she'd made about how to live. At one point her friends told her they couldn't believe that she and the "Cave Dweller" were both Christians! The other girl never seemed like she wanted anything to do with them. Thanks to Holly's courage in stepping out and living her faith in the midst of surroundings so contrary to her convictions, the girls grew more and more curious. As they became better friends, they knew they could trust her with some of their deepest struggles and questions. Holly sensed that many of them were searching, especially her roommate. Holly had been going to a church not far away and decided to invite a few of them to a service. To her surprise, they actually came! Holly walked in the door surrounded by girls, most of whom had never set foot in a church before. She sat through the service praying they weren't hating it and that they would actually get something from it. Afterwards, she couldn't believe how open they were to what they just experienced. Several wanted to keep coming.

Because Holly so prayerfully walks the line of being *in* her secular college but not *of* it, she is a true light to that campus. Though it can be rough and there are times when she feels alone in what she believes, she knows God hasn't abandoned her. It is far too evident in the way He's using her to change lives.

David Crowder Band

When the David Crowder Band's fourth album, *Remedy,* released, people seemed to be talking even more about their tour than their new music. The plan was to take the band into mainstream pop and rock venues, clubs, and bars across the country. Their previous tours had brought them into churches and Christian venues, so this was a step into foreign and potentially controversial waters. Their motive was to prove that they could find God in unexpected places, not just during their weekly church services. At the concerts, they collected thousands of towels and socks for local shelters, encouraging attendees to "be the Remedy" in their local communities.

Though this tour consisted of sold-out dates, they got a lot of flak from certain Christian music followers. Some protested that the band was an utter disgrace to their faith and warned concertgoers to avoid performances that weren't "in churches and modest settings." Others remarked on "how low" supposed Christian bands can go to present the gospel. Despite these cutting comments, the response to the tour was remarkable. God was invited in and worshipped in the most unexpected places, and people who had never darkened the door of a church got to experience and come to know God.

Switchfoot

Another Christian band who has stretched its impact into the secular world is Switchfoot. I originally came to know this band through the soundtrack of the popular movie *A Walk To Remember* and was delighted to discover that they were Christians! Their songs have always struck a chord with me as they sing about the worth of our lives, how we are "meant for more," and charge us to consider who we are and the legacy we leave. Several years ago, I heard Tim Foreman (the bassist) speak about the struggle the band had when they decided to crossover from the Christian industry into the mainstream. He said so many people turned their back on them, saying they were "sellouts" who wanted money and fame at any cost. But when you examine the course of their records over the years, I am hard-pressed to find any selling out…except to God. Their message is strong and rooted in biblical truths broadcast in a language that the world can understand. I deeply admire Switchfoot's unmistakable mission to take God to an audience who had not yet heard about Him.

Candace Cameron Bure

Did any of you grow up watching the TV show *Full House*? If you did, you may remember the oldest sister, DJ, who was always getting into trouble with her sisters Stephanie and Michelle. DJ's role was played by Candace Cameron Bure, who now, several years later, is married with a full house of her own. Recently she's made her way back into the acting scene, currently appearing on an ABC Family show. Candace is also an outspoken Christian. She released a book called *Reshaping It All: Motivation for Physical and Spiritual Fitness* in which she openly discusses her struggles and how she came to know the Lord. She is well-known in the Hollywood world and has been featured in interviews all over the mainstream media. Every time she's in front of an audience, she makes it a point to make her faith in Jesus Christ known. When a Christian interviewer asked how she is dealing with being in these secular shows she said, "I truly feel that things can't change in that business unless as a Christian I am willing to go into that industry. I don't think it can change unless light goes into the darkness...so I can shine the light of Christ." She asked for prayers as she tries to serve the Lord and witness to actors and actresses who live in a culture removed from God. Ultimately, Candace said the secular entertainment industry is her mission field. "He has given me this platform and ability and I am trying to honor Him in all the ways that I can," she finished.

The Missionary

The summer before my sophomore year of high school I went on my first mission trip with my church's youth group. As we embarked on the two-week trip we piled in a bus and road-tripped from Pennsylvania to Georgia to Arizona to Colorado to, finally, Ohio. Our longest stop was in Arizona, where we stayed on an Indian Reservation to do a Vacation Bible School program for the kids.

On our way there, our youth pastor challenged us to have a mission mindset, to make the most of every opportunity. By the time we reached the reservation, each one of us was determined to serve whomever we met and reach out to those who seemed distant. *Every* conversation and action carried an intense mission mindset, as we didn't want to leave until lives were changed by Christ.

I remember thinking, *This is amazing. I want to live like this all the time!*

And then it hit me. *Wait. Why don't I?*

Missions is what we're called to. Every day. All the time. While mission trips are incredible experiences, they give the false impression that ministry is something for which you block out a week, hop on a plane, and travel to the ends of the earth. That's certainly one way to serve... but *only* one way.

> Arise, shine, for your light has come, and the glory of the LORD rises upon you. See, darkness covers the earth and thick darkness is over the peoples, but the LORD rises upon you and his glory appears over you. Nations will come to your light, and kings to the brightness of your dawn.
>
> —ISAIAH 60:1-3

I felt deeply convicted after that summer mission trip. I knew that if my youth group acted the same way in our schools as we did on our road trip, things would be *very* different. Not only would people know without a doubt that we were Christians, but they would be challenged and changed by our convictions.

Oftentimes we have the idea that the work of a missionary is done by those radical Christians who go off to Africa. But frankly, we've missed the point. You've already learned that you have a mission, right? And if you have a mission...then you are a *missionary*!

You have a call that requires you to step into the darkness of the world and be a light—a missionary—to everyone you encounter. That may mean traveling to Zimbabwe. That may mean witnessing at your school or college. That may mean being a light at your work. That may mean sharing the Lord with your waitress. Actually...it means it *all*. Whatever you do, wherever you are, you're in the middle of a mission field. There is no room for hiding. You have to be different.

Your life is a mission.

ACTION CHALLENGE

1. Examine your heart as to how you have been walking out your faith. Are you more likely to hide from the world or blend in with it? Decide on a tangible way that you can begin more boldly living out your faith this week.

2. Pray that the Lord would show you how to "walk the line" boldly yet graciously.

3. Consider your daily routine. Who do you come into contact with who doesn't know the Lord? Have you built a relationship with them? If not, start now. Ask God to open the door for you to share about Him. Pray for the person's heart. Ask for the right words to speak into his or her life. Remember...you are a missionary *everywhere* you go..

15

GOODBYE, COMPROMISE

Let's say your friend Bob walks up and offers you a free seven-day trip to the most *incredible* resort tucked away on a tropical island. The landscape is paradise and the resort is complete with lush beaches and pools, safari adventures, day trips to theme parks, unlimited access to water sports *and* sweet concerts and nightly events. But it doesn't stop there—you can bring five other people with you! Oh, and if you happen to get tired of that island, you have your own private jet that will be waiting to take you wherever you'd like for that day.

Then Jess waltzes in and says she's got a *way* better deal to offer. She hands you a ten-day pass to stay in her uncle's tool shed, convincingly remarking what an "organic" and "refreshing" experience it will be. She'll even supply the company of her pet ferret, Doomsly. Oh, and if you happen to get tired of your surroundings, there will be a tractor waiting outside to give you and Doomsly three-minute rides from one side of the yard to the other. But remember, you only get two rides a day.

I think we can all agree that Bob's offer wins hands down. While this is a ridiculous and over-dramatic example, it depicts something real that goes on in the life of every person.

You and I are faced with choices of these extreme opposites every day. Yet often, we get suckered into choosing the trip to the shed. How could this happen?

In real life, our decisions don't present themselves as blatantly as my silly example. In fact, the amazing offer is usually tucked inside a humble-looking package while the flashy, glamorous one holds the disaster. Too often we end up trading in the incredible offer for one which we will ultimately regret.

> It's a slow fade when you give yourself away… People never crumble in a day.
>
> —CASTING CROWNS,
> "Slow Fade"

This is compromise. We've all done it.

The choice is between something life-giving and something fatal. Unknowing (well, sometimes knowing), we swap the gem for trash.

Compromise is a very real battle. At times, we are faced with what we *know* is truly right and better, but take what we seem to *want* instead. We hear the whispers and warnings, but at the moment of choice we look God straight in the face as we choose something else. Though our judgment is marred, we know exactly what we're doing. We're not delirious. We have no excuses.

I know this process well because of my own times of compromise. Though in the moment it was what I thought I wanted, I always regretted it later. Nothing was ever worth turning my back on what I knew God wanted for me. The Lord has been teaching me over the years to prepare my heart *before* being faced with a compromising situation.

Hebrews 3:15 says, "Today, if you hear his voice, do not harden your hearts as you did in the rebellion." In order to guard against hardening our heart toward God in the moment, we have to pray in *advance* to keep our hearts tender and attentive to His whisper.

Deadly Compromise

Famous singer and entertainer Amy Winehouse passed away at the age of 27. She had been a known drug and alcohol abuser and the media publically exploited her struggles. Her most famous song, "Rehab," was an autobiographical song detailing her addictions and refusal to get help at a rehabilitation center. In 2008, this song earned Amy three Grammy Awards including Song of the Year, Record of the Year, and Best Female Pop Vocal Performance. "Rehab" was the defeated cry of a troubled woman who searched for a voice to tell her she was worth saving. But instead, the world applauded her defeat and gave her the highest awards for it. As she confessed to struggling with eating disorders, depression, and self-harm, she only gained more widespread popularity. The world watched as she fell apart. In the last years leading to her death, many of her shows were canceled and she was hospitalized for drug and alcohol overdoses. Though Amy's death was tragic, sadly, it didn't come as a shock to any of her followers.

> How we live our days is how we live our lives.
>
> —*ANNIE DILLARD*

It's heart-wrenching. Amy not only threw away her precious life, but was practically *encouraged* to do so. She was a talented, God-created young woman who had every reason to live. Yet somehow, though she had the world at her fingertips, she was baited into trading her platform for embarrassment, her career for addiction, her hope for despair, and her life for death. *This* was her compromise.

Amy's painful example is a reminder of the impact of our choices. She never planned for it to end this way, but her decisions, her day-by-day choices, walked her to this fate.

Beware of the Slide

Compromise doesn't only rob us of the gifts God desires to give us. Compromise steals our very souls. But it doesn't happen overnight, of course. It sneaks in without a trace and lures us down paths we never thought we would travel. Justification becomes our easy road to destruction, as little by little we let things slide. What once was shockingly wrong suddenly becomes the norm as we let it in. Who notices the violence? The sex? The twisted moral messages? This is just "the way it is."

> You hypocrites! You shut the door of the kingdom of heaven in people's faces. You yourselves do not enter, nor will you let those enter who are trying to.
>
> —MATTHEW 23:13-14

Actually, it's not. We've become numb.

What's wrong? What's right? Our culture says that *you* get to decide. It erases our conscience and replaces it with the spineless justification—"It may be wrong for *them,* but it's okay for me."

Perhaps some of you have kept firm boundaries you believe you wouldn't cross. You may say, "I would *never* do that!" Even so, Scripture warns, "if you think you are standing firm, be careful that you don't fall!" (1 Corinthians 10:12).

Culture finds a way to glamorize the things that are most deadly to us. One little decision, and then another, and then one more add up and can lead to that fall we thought we were being so careful to avoid.

Every day, every moment, we are choosing to follow God or the world. Every one of those moments count. And what's the cost of a missed opportunity? Missing out on the adventure and the blessing of running the race He marked out for you, and only you.

A Date with Hypocrisy

When we talk about compromise, hypocrisy is at the heart of the issue. While our mouths say we desire *this,* our actions reveal we desire *that,* creating a double standard that we can't explain. A survey in the book *unChristian* by David Kinnaman and Gabe Lyons reveals that 85 percent of young non-Christians believe that present-day Christianity is hypocritical. Even worse, 47 percent of young *churchgoers* agreed.

Even Gandhi asserted that "I like your Christ; I do not like your Christians. Your Christians are so unlike your Christ."

Christians are known for their hypocrisy? What, exactly, has gone wrong here?

Online social media sites offer a very open display of our personal lives. In addition to the pictures and status updates, there's always a place to list your religious views. This often does Christianity a disservice. It lets people casually type in "Christian" without thinking anything of it…and then post the most foul words and images.

How are we representing ourselves? More importantly, how are we representing our *God*?

Most people who don't know God base their perceptions of Him on how His followers act. When we wear the name *Christian* yet live a life completely contrary to the Gospel, it sends the world a disturbing message about God. The stark reality is this: if we're going to live in blatant rebellion to the things God has called us to, He'd rather we not call ourselves Christians at all.

More Than Pretty Words

We're all guilty of putting God in a box separate from how we talk, how we dress, what we think, and what we do. Perhaps this is why the world doesn't see the point of being a Christian. When it comes to everyday life, they often can't see how we're any different.

When Christians don't represent Christ with their lives, the world is left wondering if Jesus is really in the business of changing lives at all.

I am floored by the number of Christians who apparently think cursing, trash talking, and gossiping are okay. The Bible calls the

> The greatest single cause of atheism in the world today is Christians, who acknowledge Jesus with their lips and walk out the door and get on with their lifestyle. That is what an unbelieving world simply finds unbelievable.
>
> *—BRENNAN MANNING*

power of our tongues a fire, a world of evil that corrupts the whole person and sets the whole course of our life ablaze. It goes on to say, "With the tongue we praise our Lord and Father, and with it we curse human beings, who have been made in God's likeness. Out of the same mouth come praise and cursing. My brothers and sisters, this should not be. Can both fresh water and salt water flow from the same spring?" (James 3:9-11).

Scripture has some pretty strong things to say about our tongues. If we are Christians, we *cannot* have filth pouring from it. Our words put everything at stake. James declares, "Those who consider themselves religious and yet do not keep a tight rein on their tongues deceives themselves, and their religion is worthless" (James 1:26).

Their religion is worthless.

Is that what we are suggesting with our lives and our speech? That our religion is worthless?

One of my favorite songs is called "Say Your Prayers" by the band The Wedding. The chorus of the song proclaims these words as though God is speaking them to us directly:

> You wanna walk with Me, do ya?
> You wanna walk with Me?
> Well if you love Me then just love Me,
> don't you give Me pretty words.
> Lay your life down at the altar,
> let Me see how serious you are.

These words stop me in my tracks, begging an answer to the question, "What am I truly living out?" They remind me that God knows my heart, and He demands my life. The battles we face with compromise challenge us to see whether we are *really* genuine about living for God. Have we laid down our life at His altar?

Let's see how serious we are.

Trading in for More

What is it about college, especially, that can lead so many people astray? While some people start their rebellion in high school, others remain innocent and strong in their morals until they are suddenly released to the "freedom" of a university world. I have curiously watched as friends entered into their semesters, and while some remained steadfast and matured in the Lord, far too many others left their faith at home. It's as if they decided this was their chance to "experiment." They believed their morals and faith would still be waiting at home if they wanted them, but for now it was time to live it up!

I've witnessed the changes that occur in a person who goes into their young adult years this way. It is as if they walked away as a rare, polished gem and returned as a dirtied piece of coal. Their words and way of thinking is rearranged. The truth they once believed as fact is now considered an opinion…or worse yet, a *question*. Though they entered college believing they would exit a more complete, prepared-for-life person, they discover they feel even more lost than when they began. What many don't realize when they enter the university world is the pressure they are up against. There are schools, even some that claim to be "Christian," that are indoctrinating their students with unbiblical philosophies. If young people aren't already strong in the Truth when they begin college, they can easily be swept away.

A recent Barna Group survey shows that 60 percent of twenty-somethings say that they were involved in church as a teenager but no longer attend. Only 20 percent of young adults maintain the same level of spiritual activity during their twenties that they did during their teenage years.

What is it that happens during these years?

So many members of our generation walk away from God, not realizing that this time—right here, right now—is the most pivotal time in our lives! *This* is when we lay the foundation for the rest of our lives. This is not a time to build regret and carelessly experiment; it's a time to build character and strength to start the mission God has called us to!

C.S. Lewis sums it up best when describing the irony of compromise in comparison to what God has offered us. "We are half-hearted creatures," he says, "fooling about with drink and sex and ambition when infinite joy is offered us, we are like ignorant children who want to continue making mud pies in a slum because we cannot imagine what is meant by the offer of a vacation at the sea. We are far too easily pleased."* Truly, when we choose everything *but* God, we have no idea what we're missing.

James 4:4-6 calls us out, saying, "You're cheating on God. If all you want is your own way, flirting with the world every chance you get, you end up enemies of God and his way. And do you suppose God doesn't care? The proverb has it that 'he's a fiercely jealous lover.' And what he gives in love is far better than anything else you'll find" (MSG).

One of the beautiful things about the Lord is that whenever He commands us *not* to do something, it's only because He has so much more He wants to give. The idea that God doesn't want us to have fun or be happy is beyond ignorant. God created fun. He made all the wonderful things in this life that the world has twisted for its own cause. He doesn't tell us to save sex for marriage to make us miserable, but for our own protection and our deepest fulfillment. He doesn't warn us about getting drunk to be legalistic, but so we don't foolishly loose our heads and do things we'll regret.

There is a reason behind every one of God's laws and commandments. And whatever the reason, you can trust that it's for our own good and His glory.

Colossians 3:5-17 talks about taking off our "old self" and its evil desires and replacing it with a new self that is being renewed in the image of its Creator. The passage goes through a list of actions and habits related to our sinful nature that we must "put to death" in ourselves. But it doesn't leave us there. See, it's not just about what we take off...it's about what we put on. As we take off sexual immorality, impurity, lust, evil desires, greed, anger, rage, malice, slander, lies, and filthy language, we must *put on* compassion, kindness, humility, gentleness, patience, peace, thankfulness, love, and forgiveness.

Everything God calls us to leave behind He will replace with something better.

---

* C.S. Lewis, *The Weight of Glory* (New York: HarperCollins, 2001), 26.

Kicking Compromise to the Curb

After all these years of being used and abused by compromise, it's time we finally kicked it to the curb! You and I have better things in store. Much like breaking off a bad relationship, we must remove the source of the hurt completely from our lives. But this isn't all. In order to protect ourselves, we must secure a barrier for the future.

We must guard our hearts.

Compromise begins when we allow ourselves to be weakened by not protecting our hearts from harmful things. In today's world, it is a constant, raging battle to guard our hearts. Not only guarding them in purity of body and mind, but in truth and purpose and value. As we're in the world, everything around us wars to strip us of the promises the Lord has for us.

The Message translation of Proverbs 4:23-27 tells us, "Keep vigilant watch over your heart; that's where life starts. Don't talk out of both sides of your mouth; avoid careless banter, white lies, and gossip. Keep your eyes straight ahead; ignore all sideshow distractions. Watch your step, and the road will stretch out smooth before you. Look neither right nor left; leave evil in the dust."

Our heart is where life starts—it is meant to be a well springing up with the living water that Jesus pours into us. This water is not merely meant to flow in, but stream out.

In order to live our mission in a way that impacts the world and truly represents Christ, we can't be hindered by the compromise and destruction of our flesh. Scripture says we are not to be naïve to the world, just wisely set apart from it. "I am sending you out like sheep among wolves. Therefore be as shrewd as snakes and as innocent as doves," Jesus tells us in Matthew 10:16.

The world is full of tricky schemes to keep you from living out the mission that God has given you. Be encouraged: with God, the victory is already yours. Claim it! Receive it. Compromise no longer. You, beloved of the King, have a heavenly destiny to live out. You are not bound by the chains of this world or hindered by its limitations.

Dear friends, may you never settle for less. God's best for us never has room for compromise, but requires that we give all we have to Him that we, in turn, might receive all He has for us.

ACTION CHALLENGE

1. Reflect on any areas of compromise that may have seeped into your life. Ask God to reveal the ones you may not even be aware of.

2. Write down the compromise you have found in your life and resolve to remove it. Whether it is ridding yourself of a bad habit, filthy language, inappropriate clothing, raunchy CDs, movies, books, or magazines, or whatever God leads you to, don't hesitate to throw them in the trash. Remember, everything God calls us to leave behind He will replace with something better.

16

GETTING REAL

As you read this chapter, it's my prayer that you would come to rest in who God made you to be. We live in a world of striving, but here, I want you to find safety. This chapter is about getting real, and being who you truly, beautifully are.

The Awkward Date

If you've ever been on a casual date, you know how awkward they can be. Once I went out for coffee with a guy who I knew was a great person, but when I got there, our conversation was nothing but stressful. Instead of putting me at ease, his presence made me crawl out of my skin with self-consciousness. For whatever reason, I was unable to relax and just be myself. After it was over, I felt the biggest surge of disappointment and frustration wash over me. *Why was it so hard to just be me?*

When I met my future husband, Chris, the whole experience was very different. His presence made me feel at home. His witty sense of humor and sweet, humble nature showed me that I was safe. It didn't matter if I tangled my words or tripped over my feet. He wasn't judging me…he *enjoyed* me. The thing that I found most shocking was that the more that I showed my true self, the more he seemed to love it. There was no striving. I could just be me.

So often we run the hamster wheel of trying to please. We want to be everything to everyone, yet end up feeling like nothing to anyone. We're either too much or not enough—is there an in-between? Which person should we be what for? The striving cycle never ceases.

As we seek to take our God-given mission into the world, it is essential that we do it with our true selves. God didn't make you to be someone else. The mission He assigned you has to be lived out by the raw and real you.

Living authentically includes getting real about our insecurities, wounds, fears, and imperfections. These, of course, are the very things we've become so good at hiding. After all, we've been socially trained to conceal them. What we don't realize is what a rare and precious gift they become when we genuinely and humbly reveal them. There is no shame in who you are.

No More Hiding

I have a scar.

It's ugly. It's long. It's on my right leg, and it will never go away. I used to try to hide it, and sometimes I still do.

The truth is that I'm afraid.

I'm afraid that people will look at me and only see my scar. That somehow, the rest of me will be completely overshadowed by this massive imperfection engraved on my leg, a leftover from surgery.

When I was around my nurses and doctors in the hospital, they didn't think twice when they saw my leg. In their profession, scars like mine were totally normal. However, as I began to heal and wear shorts in public for the first time after surgery, I was greeted with a very different response. People would look at my face first and smile—no problem. Then they'd glance down and gasp. When they saw my scar, their smile was choked out by horror. It broke my heart. I remember coming home in tears after that happened far too many times in one day. "Why can't they just see *me*?" I'd cry. "*I'm* not my scar!"

Somehow, in those momentary glances, I felt judged. I felt looked-over, summed-up, and thrown into some unwanted category. I was so scared of people's reactions that I started hiding my scar altogether. While I wanted to blame my insecurity on other people, it was really my own pride that had me so tangled up and convinced I couldn't display my imperfections.

Over time, God showed me that I was robbing others and myself when I hid my scar. During those times when I actually chanced revealing it, God would take over and use that moment in the most powerful way. Sure, I got comments from people who were bold (or insensitive) enough to exclaim, "Duuude, what happened to your leg?" But even that was an open door. What I had to realize was that it's not about me—it's about what *He* has done!

When I hide my scar, I hide the testimony God has given me. When I hide my scar, I hide His miraculous power. When I hide my scar, I hide His glorious story.

As I complained to God of my unwanted imperfection, He swiftly brought 2 Corinthians 12:9-10 to my mind: "He said to me, 'My grace is sufficient for you, for my power is made perfect in weakness.' Therefore I will boast all the more gladly about my weaknesses, so that Christ's power may rest on me. That is why, for Christ's sake, I delight in weaknesses, in insults, in hardships, in persecutions, in difficulties. For when I am weak, then I am strong."

> Strengthen your feeble arms and weak knees. "Make level paths for your feet," so that the lame may not be disabled, but rather healed.
>
> —HEBREWS 12:12-13

If God is truly the strongest in our weakness, then how beautiful it is to be imperfect! My scar, your scar, is His strength made visible in us.

We all have scars. Mine happens to be visible, yours may not be. Either way, it's time to stop hiding.

Playing Perfect

If you and I were to sit down together and talk, what would you want me to know about you? How would you like to come across?

Each of us, unknowingly, builds up a persona that we try to portray at all times. We create it with the way we dress, the way we talk, and the way that we present ourselves. That persona is the "ideal" you or me—what we find cool and impressive. We work hard to maintain this charade.

But what if you were sitting with Jesus? What would you have to say then? He knows you. He sees through to who you really are. It doesn't matter how cool and put-together you try to appear on the outside; all He cares about is what's within.

I remember hearing a story once about a man who took great care in cleaning a cup. This man worked hours each day to keep the outside of the vessel spotless. One day he had a visitor, and he offered him a drink from the prized cup that he kept on display. When the visitor went to take a drink from it, he practically spewed the beverage all over the man's face! The inside was filthy! The man took so much care of how the cup looked on the outside that he never considered the condition of the inside.

Jesus told a similar analogy about the Pharisees when He saw how carefully they maintained their righteous appearance, not even noticing the scum in their hearts. He told them to first clean the inside of the cup, and the outside would reflect that inner cleanliness (Matthew 23:25-26).

While the world only cares about the external, we serve a God who looks to what is *eternal*. Our messy insides are what matter most, and what He deeply wants us to expose.

Some of us hide behind the façade we've built up because we're afraid of our past. We think, *If they only knew who I was, what I've done…*Some of us hide our deep insecurity and mask it with a confident smile. Many of us have something we're trying to prove—for something, for someone. Here's what God has to say about that: "Forget the former things; do not dwell on the past. See, I am doing a new thing! Now it springs up; do you not perceive it? I am making a way in the wilderness and streams in the wasteland" (Isaiah 43:18-19).

Don't let your heart be troubled any longer by the things in your past! God doesn't want you to be trapped in shame that keeps you locked up. None of us is perfect. There is freedom in knowing we are all deeply broken people who are offered the chance to be restored. How silly to try to play perfect!

The Scent of Fakes

Our generation hates fake. We can smell it from a mile away. We find concerts that are stripped down and raw cooler than gimmicky smoke and light shows. Sure, we are still awed by the flashy stuff…but things we find legit are things we see as *real*.

In order to step out with any voice for our faith and mission, we have to—we *must*—be real. This means our faith has to be genuine to us. We can't just talk about Jesus and not walk like Him—we have too much damage to undo because of those living that way already. The world can't afford another fake.

When we are not ashamed to share our personal battles and turn to the Lord in the midst of them, we prove our faith as genuine. People want to know they are not the only ones struggling. By revealing our real selves, they in turn see a real God—a God who can comfort and restore tangible pain.

Which Self?

So, how can we be real? We hear the obvious answer all the time, "Just be yourself!" But the obvious answer must not be that helpful if we're still left struggling. It leaves us asking, *which self?* Is it the self that is most accepted? Is it the self that you'd like to be? Is it the self that you're not proud of? Which self is the real you?

> See, I have engraved you on the palms of my hands.
> —*ISAIAH 49:16*

Let's get back to the basics—the root of who you are. God has given you life, and in this life He's been writing your story. This story includes ups and downs, accomplishments and failures, joys and hurts, love and loss. These events have shaped you. It's brought you to an understanding of God and certain ideas about life. It's given you a passion and now a mission that you are called to live out. Interwoven are the personality and gifts that God handcrafted in you. These are filled with quirks and brilliance, strengths and weaknesses, likes and dislikes. Strip away the world's expectations and only measure yourself by God's. That's where you'll find yourself again.

Use What You've Got

The most powerful thing you can do is show the real you that God created. Your life is a platform, a witness, a living testimony. Use what He's given you to live your faith genuinely in the world.

Here's how you can share the real you with the world:

Through your story. This is your firsthand account of God's work in your life. It's the most powerful, authentic evidence of God that you have to offer. You can talk all day about what you believe, but your story is the *proof.* What you have gone through and the ways that you've experienced God are completely unique to you. No one else has your story.

When you share your story, others find rest and hope for themselves. Think of how you've been encouraged by someone else's testimony! Think of the ways that it inspired you and brought reality to God's promises in every situation.

As you share your story, you graciously entrust the listener with a piece of yourself. It's a precious gift, because the transparency costs you. But this is what the world craves...something *real.*

Through your mission. Your mission is an undeniable part of you that is intertwined with your passion. This is your purpose—what you were created for—and that alone will draw people. As others see you live out a great call, they will wonder where such a mission came from.

Share your passion with others. Let them know why you're doing what you're doing and what led you to it! Inform them, include them, inspire them! Let your mission ignite their own.

As you walk the set-apart road that God's mission will lead you on, the world will see the seriousness with which you live out your call. There is nothing generic about your path. When you follow it, the real you will be unmistakable.

Through your resources. Whatever country you are in, whatever your environment, speak to people in a way to which they can relate. If they've experienced trouble, seek to understand what they're going through. If you've been through hardship, use that to share your heart with them.

Thanks to constantly evolving technology, our social reach is now unlimited. With the Internet we can reach almost any part of the world. Most people are connected with a form of social media where they share their information with friends and others. We mustn't waste this outlet merely on pictures of our dogs or updates on what we're eating. This is a platform to share Christ with the world! Let every word and picture you post represent the Lord and the person He has created you to be.

Begin to see all that is around you as a resource. Consider how you can use everything in your life to genuinely live out your faith and mission.

The Reason Why

Often, we think we need permission to set our souls loose—to let what's inside venture out. We feel it's too dangerous to send our insecurities, imperfections, and shortcomings out into the world.

But there is a reason that you can rest in who God has made you to be. There is a reason that you can share your failures without being swallowed by shame. There is a reason that you can accept restoration without hiding your need.

The reason is because you are *free*.

Christ made you to have a relationship with Him and, in turn, impact the world. He didn't go to all the trouble of creating you specifically different from everybody else just to have you succumb to the pressure of fitting in the world's box. But most of all, He didn't die for you to stay chained. Jesus died to set you free.

ACTION CHALLENGE

1. Write in a journal (or a private place just for you) some things in your life that you've been hiding. Perhaps, like me, it is an imperfection that you'd prefer others not see. Perhaps it's a dark secret that you've kept hidden. Perhaps it's a struggle that you've been fighting alone. Whatever it is, write it down.

2. Find a trusted person and share what you've been hiding. If it is a battle you're fighting, seek help for it. If it's a secret from your past, throw off the burden of it. If it's an imperfection you're ashamed of, let others love you through it.

3. Pray for God to release you from these things in order to be who He has created you to be. Let Him set you free.

4. In what areas of your life has God given you victory? Perhaps it's time to share your testimony with the world.

17

WELCOME TO
THE WORLD

Somewhere in the world today a girl stands behind a window with a red light flashing, letting the passersby know she is for sale. Her body is displayed for all eyes to see, and her price tag is worn instead of her soul. It is not by choice that she stands near-fully exposed in the window, forced to give in to the demands of the man who pays to use her. She is a slave to prostitution. Having been abandoned as a child, she was left to fend for herself. Growing up, she was deceived by a man in a suit who offered her a "job opportunity." Desperate and naïve, she believed him when he promised a better life. When she stepped off the plane to be taken to her job, her passport, her belongings, and everything she had was stripped from her. She was driven to a suspicious-looking building where men forcefully led her to a small, dingy room that would become her "office." Her new wardrobe of stripper clothes stared back at her on the bare mattress. After refusing to comply and fighting to be released, she soon realized it was no use. They had taken everything. They owned her, and made sure she knew she would not escape.

This girl's story is like that of many others. She is a victim of the world's fastest growing criminal industry: sex trafficking. This is a modern-day form of slavery. Victims of sex trafficking can be women or men, girls or boys, but are most typically women and girls. Many are lured into slavery by the promise of employment or a marriage proposal. Some are sold into the bondage of the sex trade by parents, husbands, or boyfriends. Some are kidnapped by sex traffickers. Sex traffickers typically impress something called debt-bondage on their victims, telling their victims they owe money (usually for their living expenses, new "attire," and transport into the country) and must commit their personal services to pay back the debt. Traffickers also use conditioning methods such as beatings, physical torture, gang rape, confinement, starvation, forced drug use, and threats of violence to the victims and their families in order to make victims submit to their demands. While sex trafficking is a rampant issue that enslaves millions of people worldwide, it is also a growing industry in America. Currently, there are an estimated 300,000 young girls being trafficked in the United States alone. In countries where prostitution is legal, victims receive no help from their government. Victims must be rescued and aided in escape by an outside source like a daring individual or an organization or ministry which is dedicated to seeing victims freed. These precious women and young girls need to be fought for, not sold.

Just to Find Home

Somewhere in the world today there's a teenage boy who's been trapped in a gang. He lives in the city, and though he has parents and a place to live, home life is not easy. His dad is abusive and an alcoholic, and his mom is too distressed and distracted to give him attention. The neighborhood he lives in is controlled by gangs and violence is the norm. He used to walk to school terrified every day, not knowing if he'd get beat up or even killed along his route. That was, until he joined the gang. Now *he's* the one people are afraid of. His position has earned him respect and a "don't mess with me" title. The gang has become his family—the place where he fits. The members are loyal to one another and have each other's back…or so he thinks.

As he enters their system, they insist he begin to sell drugs. After all, he has to start making his share of money for the gang. Violence becomes a daily way of life. He's shot at and shoots back. His heart has become cold and hardened by the inhumane things he's seen and been assigned to do. His delusional mind whispers that it doesn't really matter whether he kills someone or is killed himself. What is he living for? The gang is the only family he knows.

Gang violence is in every major city and many of their surrounding areas. For those who grow up around it, gang violence is just a way of life. For children who grow up in families with gang members, guns are as common as toys. Some gang members have joined when they're as young as ten years old. There are many different induction methods, but one of the most common is being "jumped in." This means enduring a beating from some of the gang members for a period of time. If you can handle the beating, you're in.

The desire for respect is what drives gang life. For many members, gaining respect means committing violent crimes. Once you are part of the gang, the only way out is death or life in jail. Many members have shared their stories from prison, looking back with the deepest regret for having traded in what their life could have been for a gang. They had been looking for a family, but they ended up alone. If only they had been rescued as a child from such a life-altering decision…

Starving for Hope

Somewhere in the world today there is a child who doesn't know what it means to have hope. Her stomach is empty, and she spends her days caring for her brothers and sisters. There are seven in her family, and they all share a tiny, one-room home made out of mud, sticks, and cardboard boxes. They have one old mattress that was given to them years ago, but only the youngest children get to sleep on that. She is the oldest, and sleeps on the dirt ground next to her mother. There is no plumbing or electricity in her village, let alone her house, so every ounce of water that is used for cooking, washing, or drinking must be collected from the nearest well. This responsibility is on her shoulders.

Each day, she wakes up early in the morning to walk for miles to get the water. The trek back is by far the worst since the weight of the water nearly crushes her at every step. No matter how early she leaves home, it seems it is never early enough to escape the scorching sun. She makes up games in her mind to try and distract herself from the treacherous walk. She must stay alert, however, because this route is dangerous—the terrain is rough and predators hide in the secluded areas. The women and children who walk these routes are in constant fear of being attacked and raped. Where she lives, there is no safety. No locks on the door for protection. No cell phones to dial 911. She doesn't know the shelter of a father because he is hardly ever around. When he leaves to try to find work, he often doesn't come back for days…and even then, he rarely returns with money. Disease is rampant in the girl's village and there's not a person within it who hasn't lost a loved one. Her heart is forever scarred from watching her little sister die of starvation in her mother's arms. This is the life she knows. There is no education, no word of a Savior to show her hope…and there won't be until someone intervenes.

> I, the LORD, have called you in righteousness; I will take hold of your hand. I will keep you and will make you to be a covenant for the people and a light for the Gentiles, to open eyes that are blind, to free captives from prison and to release from the dungeon those who sit in darkness.
>
> —ISAIAH 41:6-7

Half of the world's population lives on less than two dollars a day. My drink from Starbucks costs more than that. More than six million children die each year from preventable deaths. This would be you and me, had we been born in their area.

The reality of poverty is so huge it is hard to grasp. The fact is, if we have a roof to sleep under and food in our fridge, we are rich. It's hard to imagine that we are actually in the minority of people who have that!

But the true tragedy of poverty isn't merely the lack of material things—it's the *lack of hope*. When people don't even have the most basic necessities to survive, they feel helpless. When people can't find a job to put food on their family's table, they give up. When there's so much violence that they can't protect themselves, they shut down. When there's no one to help them start a better life, they are trapped. When they've never heard the Gospel of Jesus Christ, their soul is dead.

This is the true tragedy of poverty. But it doesn't have to be that way.

The Stolen Child

Somewhere in the world today there is a father whose children have been stolen. Warlords broke into his house during the night and captured his daughter and two sons. They have been abducted to become child soldiers. The reality that awaits them is too sickening to imagine. Within the barracks they are taken to, they are completely indoctrinated and brainwashed. They are given a gun that is taller than they are and forced to kill others—sometimes their closest friends. Even the father's life is in danger. Sometimes the children are forced to go back and murder their own families. If they don't, they are killed. Some of them choose that fate.

While some child soldiers are kidnapped from their homes, others are threatened after seeing a family member murdered. Some children volunteer to join the militias, thinking it's the only way to survive in their war-torn country. They can be as young as seven years old when they are recruited. Being so young, they are vulnerable and easy to manipulate. As a CNN article wrote, "Without intervention, they could grow up to become a lost generation of migrant professional killers."* These are children whose lives have been stolen from them. This *must* be stopped.

Up Against Lies

Somewhere in the world today there is a girl who believes she is ugly. She looks in the mirror and hates what stares back at her. With every ounce of her soul she wishes she could disappear. She believes

---

* "Stolen Kids Turned into Terrifying Killers," Ann O'Neill, CNN, February 12, 2007, http://www.cnn.com/2007/WORLD/africa/02/12/child.soldiers/index.html.

she could never be thin enough, tall enough, graceful enough, pretty enough to be accepted. Even as a child, her mother always proclaimed the ways she didn't measure up…how she is worthless, good for nothing, impossible to love. If her own mother can't love her, she thinks, who can? Her loneliness and pain are too much to bear. Every advertisement, magazine cover, and image on the TV reminds her how far she is from beautiful. Culture makes it clear what guys "really" want, and it's obvious it could never be her. Constantly paranoid about her weight, she counts every calorie and even starves herself from meals when she feels she's gone over her limit. Sickness and hunger creep through her body in her attempt to gain control. Thoughts of suicide slip through her mind as she wonders, *Would anyone even notice? Would anyone even care?*

This story is right on our doorstep. It may even be *your* story. The pressure of the airbrushed images in media leave men and women, boys and girls crippled, knowing they will never measure up to that impossible "standard." Provocative images and behaviors are marketed as a goal to aspire to, but all they really do is devalue and destroy. Couple the demoralizing influence of media with the abuse of a person's parent or family member and you've got a severely wounded individual. Eating disorders, cutting, and suicide are too common. Countless stories reveal victims beginning self-harm as mere children. How ironic that so much of the world is starved for food, while others starve themselves because of the pressure of their image.

What do you do when the only thing you've ever been told is *You're worthless*? What do you believe when the only thing you've been fed are lies? *Someone* needs to bring them the truth…

More Precious Than Life

Somewhere in the world today there is a church gathering underground in a secret meeting place. Their country strictly opposes Christianity and they can be imprisoned and even killed if they are merely *caught* with a Bible. Every single day they follow Christ they risk their very lives. There are some who discreetly meet in homes to study God's word and pray—but the timing of their arrival must be carried out with absolute precision. One person is instructed to enter the house at a time, while the next must wait 45 minutes to an hour before arriving. One by one, each person enters the secret meeting place at their allotted time in order to not draw attention to the officers who are keenly looking for suspects. If they don't carry out the meeting of their Bible study just right, the building could be raided. They could be killed on the spot or carried off to prison.

There are countless stories of Christians who have been and are being persecuted for their faith. Many have ended their lives as martyrs, while some have miraculously escaped. The beauty of their stories is their unbelievable faith. Even in the face of death, they count God as more real, more valuable than even their own life. They would risk it all just for five minutes of reading His Word. The reality of this jabs me as I think of the times I "haven't found" five minutes to read my Bible.

I once heard the story of a man who was imprisoned for his faith and assigned to clean toilets in the prison. The leaders of his country had such hatred for Christians that they would rip out pages of the Bible to use as toilet paper. When the man was arrested, his Bible was taken from him. As he began to clean the toilets, he noticed the soiled pages of Scripture in the waste buckets beside them. Every day that he cleaned, he picked out those pages from the waste and carefully wiped off the excrement so that he could read the Scripture. He hid the recovered pages in his clothes and collected as many as he could find each day. What great lengths this man went in order to have even one page of the Book that at times collects dust on our bookshelves.

Christians are being persecuted all over the world. We need to be a voice for the prisoners who are in chains. They need our prayers and help as they suffer in the name of our Lord.

Fighting Alone

Somewhere in the world today there is a child who is fighting for her life…alone. When I was in the hospital, I met a little girl named Esmeralda. She was about three years old and the cutest thing I had ever seen. Esmeralda was fighting cancer, so she was bald and often sick from the chemotherapy. Her cancer was different from mine, as she had a tumor on her spine. This caused issues that made her have to wear a special brace around her midsection to keep her sitting up straight. I always felt terrible that she had to wear that big plastic case around her torso—it looked so uncomfortable. While it was hard to see such a young child suffer, the thing that disturbed me most was that she was always by herself. When I stayed at the hospital, my mom was *always* with me. My dad visited every day after work. My sisters and brothers drove all the way from college. But Esmeralda hardly ever had anyone. Once in a while I saw a young lady there who I suppose was her mother…but that was once or twice a week at most. I could see a sadness in the little girl's countenance that was different from that of the other children on our floor. She was fighting for her life on her own. There was no one there, besides the nurses, to make her smile, hold her hand when it hurt, or give her a hug at the end of the day. This kind of pain didn't seem fair.

> Learn to do right; seek justice. Defend the oppressed. Take up the cause of the fatherless; plead the case of the widow.
>
> —ISAIAH 1:17

Esmeralda, though so young, had already learned to keep people at arm's length. It took me a while to build trust and form a relationship with her, but one day she actually let me into her room to play and hang out with her. I still remember the first day I made her smile. I had beaded a bracelet for her and wheeled it over to her room. Esmeralda's face lit up when I gave it to her. I ventured to ask if she would want to watch a movie together, and to my delight she nodded her head. We made our own little theater in her hospital room, and from then on we were friends. She smiled every time she saw me, and we played together every time we were both well enough.

About a year later, after I had been healed and was visiting the hospital for a checkup, I asked the nurses about Esmeralda. With pain in their faces, they told me that she had lost her fight. It was around her fourth birthday. My heart was crushed as I thought of how alone she must have been. Sometimes what we need far more than medicine is a person to make us smile. Sometimes the only thing that keeps us holding on is knowing that someone's holding us. I wish Esmeralda had had that.

There are so many people fighting difficult battles, and so often fighting them alone. Whether it's disease, the death of a loved one, abuse, the loss of a job, or whatever pain is unique to them, we all need someone to stand by us through the pain. You and I need to be the visible proof that Jesus hasn't forgotten those who feel abandoned. They need to know that they have the Ultimate Healer and Friend by their side.

Walk a Mile in Their Shoes

Imagine yourself in each one of these stories. What if you were the woman tricked and sold into prostitution with no escape? What if you were the boy struggling to fit in who felt his only protection was to join a gang? What if you were the girl who watched her sister die of starvation or the man persecuted and imprisoned for his faith?

Now, let's take this a step further. What if that victim were your mom, your dad, your brother, your sister, your best friend? What if it was your own child?

The space between us and these issues melts away when they become personal. Suddenly we understand the people's desperation and the brutal reality of their situation. If these travesties were happening in our neighborhood, to someone we loved, we'd be campaigning every day, throwing our very being into the fight to see them saved and set free.

> Religion that God our Father accepts as pure and faultless is this: to look after orphans and widows in their distress and to keep oneself from being polluted by the world.
>
> —JAMES 1:27

But these stories *are* about our family. These are our precious brothers and sisters in Christ across the world. We may not know them, and they might not look exactly like us, but we owe them the very thing that Christ gave us—our lives.

It is our responsibility to see them set free.

If We Open Our Eyes

If you're feeling like this chapter has kicked you in the gut, just know that I feel the same. If, like me, you're feeling stunned, overwhelmed, and heartbroken by the things you read...*good*. We should be.

Bob Pierce, the founder of the humanitarian organization World Vision, once said, "Let my heart be broken by the things that break the heart of God." The issues that you have just read about *should* stir something deep and desperate in your soul. It should raise a righteous anger within you and leave your passion overflowing with the resolve that you have to do something.

Because, frankly, you *do*.

We can't sit on the sidelines and let these issues pass by us any longer. The problem isn't that we lack compassion. The problem is that we aren't aware enough of what is happening around us. If we are going to change the world, we need to know what's going on in it!

Too often we are oblivious to the news and current issues right outside our front door. Sure, we may hear bits and pieces and shake our heads, but most of the time we don't seek to know what's really happening beyond that. It's easier to just stick our heads in the sand and hope that the problems will go away by themselves, or hope that someone else will take care of them. "Someone should do something about that," we say when we hear difficult stories. We know the situation is heart wrenching and wrong and unjust, yet we instantly assign "someone else" to solve the mess.

> Our greatest fear as individuals and as a church should not be of failure, but of succeeding at things in life that don't really matter.
>
> —*TIM KIZZIAR*

While this book has hopefully led you on a personal discovery, there is a greater reason for this wake-up call. It's about what's going on in the world and where you fit in. It's about what God is doing and what He wants to do through you. It's about using your mist of time on earth to truly live for Christ and fulfill the needs of others.

Where You Come In

Sometimes I think about all the issues in the world and feel frustrated and overwhelmed. I can't possibly fix them all!

But this is where you come in.

You, me, the next person and the next person, each living out our God-assigned mission, *can* change the world. Each one of us has a part, and as we live out our gifts and passions, one by one these devastating needs will begin to melt away. As we impact one person, the domino effect is then spread to everyone *they* touch. The influence catches like wildfire.

My intent with this chapter isn't to leave you depressed, but to serve as a reminder that the world is so much bigger than just you or me. This world is full of all kinds of needs, but there are also all kinds of gifts, abilities, and skills within us to *serve* and *save* those people! That's the beautiful part.

When I was on a ministry trip recently, one of my group leaders told us "The Starfish Story," which was adapted from an essay by Loren Eiseley. I want to share it with you...

> One day a man was walking along the beach when he noticed a boy picking something up and gently throwing it into the ocean. Approaching the boy he asked, "What are you doing?"
>
> The youth replied, "Throwing starfish back into the ocean. The surf is up and the tide is going out. If I don't throw them back, they'll die."
>
> "Son," the man said, "don't you realize there are miles and miles of beach and hundreds of starfish? You can't make a difference!"
>
> As if he hadn't heard, the boy bent down, picked up another starfish, and threw it back into the surf. Then, smiling at the man, he said, "It made a difference for that one."

God doesn't call you to single-handedly rescue everyone; He calls you to purposefully impact *someone*.

Welcome to the world. It needs you.

> The Spirit of the Sovereign LORD is on me,
>   because the LORD has anointed me
>   to proclaim good news to the poor.
> He has sent me to bind up the brokenhearted,
>   to proclaim freedom for the captives
>   and release from darkness for the prisoners,
> to proclaim the year of the LORD's favor
>   and the day of vengeance of our God,
> to comfort all who mourn,
>   and provide for those who grieve in Zion—
> to bestow on them a crown of beauty
>   instead of ashes,
>   the oil of joy
>   instead of mourning,
> and a garment of praise
>   instead of a spirit of despair.
> They will be called oaks of righteousness,
>   a planting of the LORD
>   for the display of his splendor
>   (ISAIAH 61:1-3).

ACTION CHALLENGE

1. Of all the examples of world needs that were shared in this chapter, which of these stories gripped you the most? Why?

2. Which issues were you already aware of? Which ones surprised you?

3. Consider the ways in which you can become more actively aware about what is going on in the world. Begin the discipline of skimming the news each day to stay informed. (I have found that making a news website my homepage when I pull up the Internet has been an awesome, easy way to stay up-to-date. Every time I open my browser, the latest news headline pops up with surrounding stories.)

4. What issue are you most passionate about? Which one relates to your personal mission? Make it a point to research what is going on in the world with that need specifically, and keep up to date on others as well. The better we know and understand the need, the better we will be able to serve.

5. Pray daily for the world need that is closest to your heart.

6. Go impact that issue in a personal, hands-on way.

18

LIVING AWAKENED

Dear friend, do you see now that your life is too valuable to be wasted?

Have you caught a glimpse of the unbridled love that your Savior Jesus has for you? Have you made peace with your wandering soul and accepted His purpose for your life? Have you rejoiced in your freedom to become exactly who He created you to be? Has your soul been ignited by the adventurous story He's writing in you? Do you see the gaping need in the world for your mission to be fulfilled?

Since the Lord first gave me the vision for this book, it has been my prayer that it would not merely leave you touched but would awaken the very depths of your being and breathe your mission into action.

If the question "Where do I start?" is bubbling up inside you, take a minute to reflect on the stories that I'm about to share. As you consider what *your* mission will look like as it is lived out in the world, let these incredible examples of those who have blazed the trail before you leave you inspired. May their radical stories set fire to your own.

Katie Davis

Katie was the homecoming queen at her high school in Brentwood, Tennessee. Only four years later, her life couldn't be more different.

When Katie was young, she always admired Mother Teresa as a role model and felt inspired by the spirit of Christ within her. At 15, Katie declared to her parents that she wanted to do missions work overseas after high school. But it wasn't until she traveled to Uganda during her senior year that she knew her heart had found home. Katie was immediately captivated by the people and culture, and was willing to drop everything in order to stay there.

That summer, God opened the door for Katie to return to Uganda and teach kindergarten at an orphanage. She told the man who ran the school that she wasn't qualified, but he didn't care. He couldn't have been more ecstatic to have someone with Katie's heart there.

Katie was expecting a class of seven students, but on the first day 138 showed up. There is no free public schooling in Uganda, and most children's families can't afford to pay. So when word got out about the new teacher in town and the free classes at the orphanage, children flooded in from every direction.

As Katie continued to work with these children, she began to see into the world of poverty like she never had before. God stirred her heart as she prayed about what she could do for the hopeless children and families she passed every day on the street. *Start a child sponsorship program,* He whispered to her.

So at the age of 19, Katie started a non-profit organization called Amazima Ministries International. Her goal was to have someone sponsor an orphaned or vulnerable child for $300 a year ($25 a month) in order to send them to school, provide supplies, give them three hot meals each day, and care for them with spiritual discipleship and medical attention. Though she only originally planned to have 40 children in the program, she now has over 400. Her organization also started a feeding program in the community that nourishes over 1,600 people each week, as well as a self-sustaining vocational program for the village's women.

But Katie hasn't stopped there. Giving to these children wasn't enough. Now, at 22 years old, she has become the mother of 14 Ugandan daughters that she adopted into her home. Her family is a vital part of the village and their house is always hosting Bible studies and caring for those in need.

When I think about this amazing young woman and the life that she leads, my heart is filled with inexpressible joy just imagining the legacy she will be leaving among countless generations. In four short years the whole village has been transformed, all because an 18-year-old girl dared to live her mission. The best part is, she couldn't be happier. *This* is what she was made for!

> Sometimes I am walking through the noisy market, down the dusty Africa road with the hotter-than-imaginable sun beating down on my face. Everyone around me is blacker than the night. Everything is beautiful. Despite the sweltering heat, I get goose bumps. I live in Africa…This is Africa and this is where I live and this is where I love. This is my place, where my heart and soul are. God has put me here, a place beyond all my dreams and imagination. I don't know why me. I don't know why anything. But I know. I am certain. This is *the plan*. This is *my place*. And tears of joy run down my face, in the hot, dusty, noisiness, because I am *home*.*

Everett Swanson

Everett was a pastor from Chicago who volunteered to go to Korea and preach to the troops during the war in 1952. He had never been to another country, but the few days that he was there changed his life.

When he first arrived a little boy ran up to him, stole his winter coat, and took off. As Everett chased after the boy to get his coat, he turned a corner and saw it lying on the ground. He thought perhaps the boy had gotten scared, dropped the coat, and run. As he picked it up, however,

---

* Katie Davis, *Kisses from Katie* (blog), September 17, 2007, www.kissesfromkatie.blogspot.com.

he discovered a frightened and terribly thin little boy shivering beneath it. Suddenly Everett looked around and began to notice the piles of rags around him—all with children huddled under them. They were starving and desperate to keep warm in the dead of winter. These children were orphans whose parents had been killed in the war. No one was there to care for them. All they had were each other and the rags they found to keep warm.

> Speak up for those who cannot speak for themselves, for the rights of all who are destitute. Speak up and judge fairly; defend the rights of the poor and needy.
>
> —PROVERBS 31:8-9

That night, Everett couldn't sleep as he thought about those little children on the street. In the morning he went back out where he had seen them the day before, only to find a garbage truck circling the area. Everett noticed the men kicking piles of rags, throwing some into the garbage and leaving others. Wondering what they were doing he approached, only to find that those piles of rags were not just rags…those were children. They were kicking the children huddled under the pieces of cloth to see who had made it through the night and who had died. Those who didn't survive were thrown into the garbage.

Everett was horrified by this discovery. His heart and stomach grew sick and he knew that something had to be done. On his plane ride home the words *What are you going to do?* haunted him, playing over and over in his mind. When he arrived back home, he told a friend about the terrible things he had witnessed and how those children needed their help. To Everett's shock, his friend wrote him a check for a thousand dollars. The friend said that God had told him to give this money to a person who wanted to help widows and orphans. So Everett took that money, and in the basement of his home he started what would become the world's leading Christian child development ministry—Compassion International.

Initially, Everett Swanson helped 35 orphaned children. Now his organization helps over 1.2 million children in 26 countries. A source from Compassion International stated, "Instead of being overwhelmed by their inability to change the life of every child, Swanson and his friends decided they would concentrate on changing the life of every child they could—one by one."

Susie Jennings

I first met Susie a few years ago after helping at a homeless event in Dallas during Christmas. This lady, though very petite, had a big presence. When I met her, I remember noticing how her joy and dynamic spirit bubbled over. She was the founder of an organization that served thousands of homeless people in Dallas. At the time, all I knew about her was that she had put together the most amazing homeless event I had ever seen. What I didn't know was the incredible story of how God brought her there.

March 9, 1993 marked the first day of the darkest season in Susie's life. Her husband, David, went missing. He had been suffering from depression, which only worsened when he lost his job and a family member close to him. During the long weeks with no trace of him, Susie was left heartsick and desperate for answers. She sought the Lord furiously through verses, hymns, and prayer. His peace was the only thing keeping her sane.

Finally, on the third week, an unexpected visitor came knocking on her door. It was a detective who had come to let her know that her husband's car had been found. Susie, her father-in-law, and her pastors went to help search for him. To her horror, a body was discovered. David had committed suicide.

Susie collapsed in shock. Despair washed over her and she cried at the top of her lungs for God to give her strength.

And He did. God brought Susie closer to Him than ever through her pain.

Three months later, Susie had a dream that she was knocking on people's doors sharing the gospel. God showed her that out of her hurt and anguish, a ministry for widows and single mothers was to be born. She organized The Lord's Bride Fellowship for widows and single moms. But that was only the beginning.

As Susie allowed God to use her in this ministry, she prayed that He would show her what she could do for Him in the community. She was driving downtown in Dallas near a bridge when she felt the Lord direct her attention to the left, where she saw more than 100 homeless men and women who were living under the bridge in cardboard boxes. Susie had been driving this exact route for ten years but had never noticed the people before. She felt the Lord telling her to go under the bridge to those people. Her initial response was, "No! Those homeless people could be violent and crazy!" But the Lord quickly reminded her, "It was you who asked what you could do for Me." Immediately she felt foolish for her response, and asked the Lord what she was supposed to bring those people. The Lord replied with one word: "Blankets."

The next day, Susie began gathering blankets from her friends and ended up collecting 100 to take down to the homeless under the bridge. As she and her friends distributed them, they shared the gospel with each person. Many of the men and women found hope in Christ that day. This work continued and expanded each month, until what started as merely 100 blankets became an organization helping thousands—Operation Care Dallas.

Now Susie's organization helps thousands of homeless men and women all over the country. Their signature event at Christmastime was the one of which I had the privilege of being a part. The event was held in the Dallas Convention Center downtown and served over 11,000 homeless men, women, and children. The organization not only provides people with food, clothes, and basic necessities, but with legal aid, job help, medical care, a chance to connect with estranged family, and counselors to sit with each person, pray for them, and share the gospel. Each year, thousands of lives are given to the Lord and completely transformed.

When I think about the incredible way that God has used Susie, I am left amazed by the way her story started. As a widow in great pain and distress, her eyes were opened to all the needs around her. Much of her healing has come through helping others. It was Susie's pain that unleashed her mission, and that mission turned pain into purpose.

Richmond Wandera

Richmond's story and life is a miracle…but you might be surprised by *how* his life was changed.

Richmond grew up in deep poverty in Africa. When he was only six years old, his father was killed and his mother was left to care for her eight children. Unable to afford to stay in their small house, they were forced to seek shelter in the country's biggest slum. All nine of them tried to pack themselves into the tiny, box-like structure that was to become their home. During this time his mother became increasingly ill, but there was no money to care for her. Richmond and his siblings were desperate. He and his sister wandered the streets to try and find food to eat. They could only survive for so long.

One day his mother told him that she had heard about an organization called Compassion International that would try to find sponsors for the children who were put on their list. There was only room for two of her children to sign up, so she chose Richmond and one of his younger sisters. The family prayed and prayed that the children would receive sponsors.

Four months later, they got news that a girl named Heather from the United Kingdom had chosen to sponsor Richmond. No words can describe the extraordinary joy that news brought into his family's home! There was rejoicing, dancing, and celebrating for days straight! Suddenly Richmond was given food for his family, healthcare, and the chance to get an education. It was the first ray of hope they had.

The biggest change in Richmond's life, however, came through Heather's letters. For years, poverty had stripped him of his dignity. It had washed away his self-worth and stolen his hope. But when Heather wrote to him, she said things like, "I love you and am praying for you," "I believe in you," and encouraged him by saying how treasured he is to the Lord. Her words brought life to Richmond in a way he never felt before. He said in an interview later, "Her letters were my most precious asset." Heather's love for Richmond, though she had never met him, helped him understand the love of a God that he had never seen. Because of this, Richmond accepted Christ at the age of 15.

But it didn't stop there. Because of the love that Richmond was shown through Compassion and Heather, his mother and four brothers accepted Jesus as Lord of their lives too.

Fast-forward a few years. Because of Compassion's leadership development program, Richmond was given the opportunity to go to college. He was also asked by his church to become the youth pastor, and eventually the associate pastor. Richmond later had the privilege of studying at the Moody Bible Institute in Chicago, Illinois. Here, he received his Master of Arts degree in Spiritual Formation and Discipleship.

Richmond is now fluent in six languages, travels the world sharing his testimony, and disciples and trains pastors in other parts of the world. His deep gratitude for having been released from the hopelessness of poverty has fueled his passion to wade right back into the need and serve others trapped there. His mission is to change his nation for the glory of Christ.

All of these things happened because of the decision of one person. Heather made the simple choice to sponsor Richmond, having no idea what kind of impact this decision would have not only on him, but his family, his country, and the world. But here's the part that you don't know about Heather…

She did this when she was a teenager.

Lindsay Giambattista

Lindsay was just a normal teenage girl who loved shopping and clothes. She was blessed to be raised in a Christian home under the loving guidance and care of her parents. Having been fairly sheltered as a child, she was removed from some of the cold realities of the outside world. It wasn't until she entered her teen years that her eyes began to open.

When her life intersected with those of at-risk girls, she was left stunned by the stories of troubled young women right in her area. These girls are left to find their own way…sometimes on the streets. They are often abandoned or abused, with no one to protect or care for them.

This realization affected Lindsay deeply. Coming from a loving home, she couldn't imagine life as these girls had experienced it—so cruel, cold, and lonely. God convicted her heart with the desire to show those girls His bottomless love. Lindsay didn't know where to start, but she prayed and prayed until she got an interesting idea.

She wondered about taking her clothes, her prized possession, and giving them to the girls who had nothing. Perhaps their common "girly" interest in clothes could be the bridge that enabled her to tell them about God's love. Excited about the idea, Lindsay shared it with friends and enlisted people to donate new or like-new clothing. Before she knew it, she had nearly 70 huge bags of designer clothes stacked floor to ceiling in her room!

What started as a neat idea turned into a much better reality. A foster care company offered space for her to build her own boutique where the girls could come in and "shop" for the clothes—for free!

Lindsay now runs the boutique that she calls Taylor's Closet, which is specifically for foster and at-risk girls. Each girl that enters has an individual appointment where she is given special care, fashion consultation, and is allowed to pick six items that are hers to keep. At the end of her makeover, Lindsay sits down with the girl to talk. As she listens to the girl's story, she shares the gospel and tells the girl how much God delights in her. Lindsay's desire is to let the girls know how valuable they are, and that they have a Father in heaven who really, *really* loves them.

For those who choose to get involved, Lindsay, her mom, and some others offer a Bible study and mentoring program. This way they can be connected to furthering the girls' walk with the Lord and encouraging them in their relationship with Him. This kind of fellowship and support is essential.

Lindsay's mom has joined her daughter in this ministry…in her own way. She's built a kitchen onto a separate part of the boutique where she teaches the girls how to prepare food. Many of them haven't had a home to cook in and have no idea how to open a can of soup or cut a tomato. It is this kind of one-on-one mentoring that shows the girls that they are truly loved, noticed, and worthwhile. It is evidence that there really is a God who cares for them.

Lindsay started this ministry when she was only 14 years old. All she had was an idea and a desire to help the troubled girls in her community. Now she has a high-end boutique where she freely gives away the things she loves: Christ and clothes.

You Don't Have to Start an Organization

Before we continue, let's just get one thing straight. These stories are examples of amazing ways that some people have and are living out their mission. They in no way are supposed to imply that you have to start an organization to live yours.

There are so many ways to go about it! Check out what these two awesome individuals did.

Greyson Holmes

Greyson had a reputation at his school as the troublemaker—the one who always goofed around. To his teachers, he was always up to something. But his senior year, he surprised them by being up to something good.

Greyson was adopted by his grandparents and attended a small Christian school. During his senior year he took a course that became one of his favorites—Contemporary Issues. He looked forward to it every day because of the relevant and inspirational subject material. When the teacher assigned the students' final class project, they were each sent to search for a nonprofit organization they believed in, give their time to it, and present their results to the class.

Greyson landed upon the Make-A-Wish Foundation. When he discovered they granted wishes to children with life-threatening illnesses, he thought it was the coolest thing he had ever heard. There was no doubt he wanted to do his project on this organization.

When he gave Make-A-Wish a call, he was disappointed to hear that you had to be 21 years old to be a wish granter. This is a person who meets with children to learn about their one true wish and to help make it the most delightful experience possible. Since Greyson wasn't old enough to help on that level, he asked what other ways he could get involved. The Make-A-Wish representative in his area assured him that there were plenty of ways, and gave him several ideas.

When the time came for Greyson to give his presentation, everyone in his class was awed by what he shared about Make-A-Wish. One of his friends was especially inspired, and came up to him after class to suggest that he put together a fundraiser for them at the school. Not having any previous experience with this sort of thing, Greyson laughed it off. But it got him thinking, and he later ran the idea by his teacher to see what he thought. Greyson's teacher loved it and encouraged him to give it a try.

Curious about where to start, he called the Make-A-Wish chapter to see what it would take to do a fundraiser. They told him the minimum amount he needed to raise would be $5,000—this is how much it costs to grant one child's wish. At the sound of that number, Greyson almost gave up before he started! He was thinking more like $500…$5,000 was a goal he wasn't sure he could pull off.

But he went ahead with it anyway. The next few weeks turned out to be some of the craziest of his life. He had no idea what kind of wild ride he had gotten himself into! Though his teachers were supportive, they let *him* do the work. Ultimately, he was glad to have the responsibility because it made him work harder to see the goal through. Initially he only let a few of his friends know what he was doing, and a couple of them committed to help. They decided that the fundraiser should be based around a basketball game with the school's biggest rival—that was sure to draw crowds from both schools. To get all age groups involved, they included a spot during halftime where the elementary kids would play, and then added a dodgeball tournament where people could pay to play after the basketball game.

Greyson had never taken on so much responsibility in his life. Suddenly he was heading up meetings, collaborating with teachers, visiting businesses to obtain donations and support, and speaking in front of large school assemblies to promote the event.

All of these things were completely foreign to him.

But as he spearheaded the cause and it gained momentum, he noticed people were quick to jump on board and excited to support it.

The real heart behind it all came from knowing the efforts and money were going to grant a wish for a girl named Jamie. She was 14 years old and suffering from leukemia. Her dream, her wish, was to go to Alaska and see the Northern Lights. Jamie was the driving force behind the whole event. Everyone wanted be part of seeing her wish fulfilled.

Finally, when the night of the game arrived, Greyson could hardly believe the line of people waiting to get into the gym—it wrapped all the way outside the school! The spirit of the crowd was alive with excitement and brimming with joy in being a part of such a great cause.

That night, Greyson was unexpectedly honored and given a standing ovation for his work in putting the event together. That was the moment when it hit him—*this was the best thing he had ever done.* That goal that he thought was impossible? He exceeded it. Instead of raising $5,000, he raised over $10,000 for the Make-A-Wish Foundation that night. This was enough to not only grant Jamie's wish, but another child's as well!

As Greyson recounted the experience, he told me how he never thought he could do something like this. It is clear that God used him to do far more than he could have ever done on his own. This has inspired Greyson to keep going and take this newfound passion onto the college campus with him. With this accomplishment under his belt, he wants to do something even bigger next.

Meredith Medlin

If Meredith could major in "helping people" in college, she would. That's what her heart loves. But since that degree isn't yet an option, she's chosen to make it her daily lifestyle.

When she was in high school, Meredith read the book *The Irresistible Revolution: Living as an Ordinary Radical*. It inspired her to engage in helping and loving those in need around her. This sparked a conversation between her and a friend about what they could do to reach out to people in their community. As they talked, Meredith said it would be awesome to go downtown and hang out with some of the homeless people. Her friend suggested that they make sandwiches and bring food. So they took their idea and got to work!

That Monday Meredith, her friend, and her friend's mom went downtown with a backpack full of sandwiches and water bottles. Each time they approached a homeless person, they were careful to treat them with the utmost respect, always calling them "ma'am" or "sir." As they gave the person food and water, they asked how they were doing and struck up a conversation. One of the things that surprised Meredith most was how much the people wanted to talk. They were so used to being brushed off and ignored, it was a joy for them to have someone want to sit and listen. Out gushed their stories, how they got to where they were, what they were working toward now, and all kinds of things. Meredith found that caring for them first with food opened the door to form a relationship and share about God.

After the first time doing this, Meredith was hooked. From then on, there was nothing else in the world that she wanted to do with her Mondays after school.

As she began to go more, some of her friends heard what she was doing and asked if they could join her. Some weeks, they had groups of teenagers as big as 15 going downtown to talk to the homeless and give them sandwiches. In those cases, they felt it was best to break into smaller groups—so they wouldn't be so overwhelming!

When Meredith started doing this, she made it her responsibility to buy the food they handed out. She worked a part-time job to cover the costs and told me that her paycheck always went to "food for the homeless and gas for my car." But as other people got involved, they began to develop a system where they would rotate buying the food and taking it downtown each week.

Meredith's idea took on such a following and developed such passion in others that when she was about to head to college, she didn't have to worry whether her ministry downtown would continue. Two younger girls at her school asked if they could take it over while she was gone. She gladly agreed!

She told me, "I love that I could start something, but that it's not *mine*. Other people have taken it and grown it, and now it's a joint effort that so many others are part of!"

Since the very first day that she and her friend brought sandwiches downtown, someone has gone downtown every single week to feed the homeless and build relationships. Rain or shine, no matter the weather, they are dedicated to serving.

> Look at the nations and watch—and be utterly amazed. For I am going to do something in your days that you would not believe, even if you were told.
>
> —HABAKKUK 1:5

"One of my favorite parts about what we do is that it's not through an organization—it's just us. That's what always surprises people when we meet them. There are no adults making us do this; we just *want* to," Meredith said.

After she and her friends meet each person, give them some food, and talk to them for a while, they ask if they can pray with them. They've been amazed to see how much more receptive the people are to hearing about the Lord *after* they've been shown care and love. It's almost like getting to see God, *then* hear about Him.

These weekly trips downtown to visit the homeless people that Meredith now calls her friends have changed her life. The joy that doing this brings her is evident—she has a glow that people only have when they've given their life to something worthwhile. This has become *her* mission—to love God, love people without bounds.

Though she would argue that serving others has blessed her more than those she's helped, perhaps one day when she gets to heaven, she'll realize that the joy that she brought the Lord was far greater than even her own.

Your Name Here

What if the next story in this book were yours? What would it look like? How would your mission be lived out? Who are the countless individuals whose lives will be changed by it?

These stories are meant to inspire you and prove that it is possible to follow God and live your mission in the face of any circumstance. No matter where you come from, who you've been, or what you have or don't have, nothing can stop you when you are connected to the source of life Himself! Our God knows no bounds.

You have a calling which you cannot ignore. There is nothing more real in life than the Maker of the Universe who created you for His plan and loved you enough to die so you could live it out. If you miss this, you miss the entire purpose of your life.

So, what will your story be?

The Awakening

I believe that you and I are living in the midst of a great awakening. I see a movement on the rise of people waking up to their God-given passion and living out His mission for their lives. I see the world being changed by ordinary individuals who become extraordinary by the Lord's strength.

My heart is filled with the utmost excitement for you and the plans God has for you. I believe that He has chosen you to write a specific piece of history. Your adventure is waiting, if you only dare to step in.

> Here is my servant, whom I uphold, my chosen one in whom I delight; I will put my Spirit on him, and he will bring justice to the nations.
>
> —*ISAIAH 42:1*

If you are holding this book in your hands, I want you to know it's not an accident. God knew every single person who would read these pages. He has planned for this very moment in your life to be a turning point, a crossroad where you only have two choices:

Will you radically serve Him with the mission He's given you?

or

Will you waste your life?

PAIGE OMARTIAN is a 21-year-old recording artist, author, and speaker whose battle with cancer as a child led her on a remarkable journey inspiring others to grasp the preciousness of life and live out their purpose. She has traveled the country sharing her music and story and was featured on Bath and Body Work's 2005 Christmas CD supporting the Make-A-Wish Foundation. Paige was interviewed on *The Today Show* and was the speaker and TV host for the ministry iShine. She released her debut rock album, *Wake Up*, in 2009. Paige and her husband, Chris, are newlyweds and live in Nashville, Tennessee.

To learn more about books by Paige Omartian or to read sample chapters, log on to our website:

www.harvesthousepublishers.com

Me when I was ten years old. Just a healthy kid without
a care in the world.

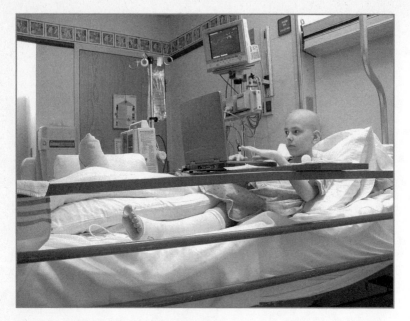

In the hospital getting treatment after my bone replacement surgery.

This was taken during my battle with cancer. Kiana, my constant companion, didn't care that I'd lost my hair from the chemotherapy.

Standing at the microphone during my wish (granted by the Make-A-Wish Foundation) to go to Nashville, Tennessee, and record in a professional studio.

Doing a TV interview during the Bath & Body Works media tour, on which I was an ambassador for the Make-A-Wish Foundation.

Standing in front of a home I visited in the Dominican Republic with Compassion International in 2011.

This is me with my friend Esmeralda. We were both being treated for cancer, but she was fighting her battle alone. This picture will always be so precious to me. I loved it when she smiled.

In the Dominican Republic loving on my brother
and sister-in-law's precious sponsor child, Rosanny.
She traveled four hours from her village to meet
me. I will never forget that experience.

Find more bonus content, pictures, and videos at
www.paigeomartian.com

Before she was PAIGE OMARTIAN, she was PAIGE ARMSTRONG...and she put out a seriously ROCKIN' ALBUM!

WAKE UP
from Whiplash Records

"Wake Up [steals the show]. Whether it's the loud stomping-on-toes of 'Apathy' or the quiet beauty of 'Unbreak Me,' you won't leave this one without a favorite track."

—Christian Music Review

"Every once in a while a CD comes along and you know it is going to quickly join your series of most-played. Paige Armstrong's debut release *Wake Up* is definitely one that will be making its way onto mine. Armstrong's sound is edgy and in-your-face with guitar and drums that don't let up and an urgency that compels listeners to take full advantage of the days and lives they have been given. Overall, *Wake Up* causes the listener to do just that—and not just with its driving guitar and amazing vocals, but with its urgent and inspiring lyrics."

—Shady Little Road Music Reviews

Stay tuned for upcoming new music from PAIGE OMARTIAN!

Want to change the world?
Start by changing the life of one person.

*J*oin me
and release a
child from
poverty in
Jesus' name!

Visit compassion.com/paigeomartian
to sponsor a child today.

**Every day, children's lives are
changed through wishes granted by
Make-A-Wish®.**

Make-A-Wish grants the wishes of children with life-threatening medical conditions to enrich the human experience with hope, strength and joy. According to a 2011 study of wish impact, most health professionals surveyed say a wish come true can affect health outcomes. Kids say wishes give them renewed strength to fight their illness, and their parents say these experiences strengthen the entire family.

**Visit Make-A-Wish at wish.org to find out how
you can get involved today.**